Ceran St. Vrain

Ceran St. Vrain

Ceran St. Vrain. Copy of a portrait taken in 1868
and given to his daughter Felicitas (courtesy Robert F. Dodson)

Ceran St. Vrain

American Frontier Entrepreneur

Ronald K. Wetherington

with
Foreword
by
Marc Simmons

SUNSTONE PRESS

SANTA FE

Sunstone books may be purchased for educational, business, or sales promotional use.
For information please write: Special Markets Department, Sunstone Press,
P.O. Box 2321, Santa Fe, New Mexico 87504-2321.

Book and Cover design › Vicki Ahl
Body typeface › Trebuchet MS
Printed on acid-free paper
∞

Library of Congress Cataloging-in-Publication Data

Wetherington, Ronald K.
    Ceran St. Vrain : American frontier entrepreneur / by Ronald K. Wetherington ; with foreword by Marc
Simmons.
        p. cm.
    Includes bibliographical references and Index.
    ISBN 978-0-86534-858-5 (softcover : alk.paper)
1. St. Vrain, Ceran, 1802-1870. 2. Pioneers--New Mexico--Biography. 3. Trappers--New Mexico--Biography.
4. Businessmen--New Mexico--Biography. 5. Flour mills--New Mexico--History--19th century. 6. Flour
mills--Colorado--History--19th century. 7. Excavations (Archaeology)--New Mexico--Taos. 8. Flour mills
--New Mexico--Taos--History--19th century. 9. Material culture--New Mexico--Taos--History--19th century.
10. Taos (N.M.)--Antiquities. I. Title. II. Title: Ceran Saint Vrain.
    F800.S7W48 2012
    338.092--dc23
    [B]
                        2011050853

WWW.SUNSTONEPRESS.COM
SUNSTONE PRESS / POST OFFICE BOX 2321 / SANTA FE, NM 87504-2321 /USA
(505) 988-4418 / ORDERS ONLY (800) 243-5644 / FAX (505) 988-1025

To Fred Wendorf
teacher, mentor, friend

Contents

Foreword

by

Marc Simmons

from

The Santa Fe New Mexican

May 16, 2009

Cerán St. Vrain, a close associate of Charles Bent and Kit Carson, ranks as a major figure in 19th-century New Mexican history. Yet today, he is unrecognized and his absorbing story goes unsung. The grandfather of Cerán was a French-speaking nobleman who served as King Louis XIV's treasurer. Revolution forced him to flee the country with his family and settle in the wilds of France's Upper Louisiana colony.

Cerán St. Vrain was born into a French-speaking community in 1802 near St. Louis. After the death of his father, he was sent as a youth to live with Bernard Pratte Sr., head of a major fur-trading company. In his early 20s, St. Vrain made his first trip to New Mexico as a merchant, carrying goods bought on credit from Pratte. He earned enough to keep him in that business for the next three decades.

In 1826, the young man, along with 35 other Americans, applied for travel permits to undertake a trading and trapping expedition to Sonora, below the Gila River. The papers were issued by New Mexico Gov. Antonio Narbona. The permit handed to St. Vrain showed his name, as Hispanicized by a clerk, to be Serán Sambrano. Thereafter, he was known to New Mexicans as Señor Sambrano.

The Sonora trip indicates that St. Vrain was on his way to becoming a full-fledged mountain man as well as a merchant. The following year, 1827, he participated in a nine-month trapping expedition northward to the Platte River and then west to the Green River.

S.S. Pratte, a kinsman of St. Vrain's old St. Louis benefactor, led the party. Along the way, the leader was bitten by a mad dog and soon died in agony from the infection. A grieving St. Vrain sat by his side until the end. Against his wishes, he was voted by the men to become their new leader.

Over the next several years, St. Vrain divided his time between selling imported goods in Santa Fe and Taos and trapping beaver. He established a residence in Taos, became a naturalized citizen of Mexico (whose territory then extended north to the Arkansas River), and got married to a local girl. He also mastered the Spanish language.

In addition, he began to develop a large Mexican land grant. Known as the Vigil and St. Vrain grant (also called the Las Animas grant), it had been awarded by Gov. Manuel Armijo. The tract sprawled across 4 million acres in southeast Colorado.

Around 1832, St. Vrain formed a partnership with another trader, Charles Bent, also from St. Louis. Bent, St. Vrain & Co., in the words of historian Hiram Chittenden, "became one of the most important fur-trading firms in the West." The following year, the partners built Bent's Fort on the Arkansas River, near modern La Junta, Colo. Although they had stores in Santa Fe and Taos, the fort, which purchased furs from mountain men and buffalo robes from Plains Indians, became the headquarters of their mercantile empire.

St. Vrain spent most of his time there, dressed in a frock coat and tie, keeping the firm's books. But he switched to fringed buckskins when going forth to deal with the trappers.

Early 1847 saw the killing of Charles Bent in the bloody Taos disturbances. St. Vrain happened to be in Santa Fe and accompanied the army that put down the uprising. Afterward he served as the interpreter for some of the rebels who were placed on trial. Bent, St. Vrain & Co. dissolved and with New Mexico now in American hands, St. Vrain entered upon a series of diverse ventures that would make him a wealthy man. Initially, he sold off pieces of the huge land grant, his partner Corelio Vigil having perished at Taos along with Bent. Then he got interested in milling and built the first grist mill in the Taos Valley, and others in Mora, Santa Fe and Peralta, below Albuquerque. By selling flour to the new army garrisons at Fort Union and Fort Craig, he made enormous profits.

For the rest, Señor Sambrano invested in sawmills, became involved in banking projects and early railroad speculation, and owned a share of the capital's *Santa Fe Gazette*. For a time he dabbled in territorial politics. The last years of his life were spent in Mora in an adobe house with a placita, located in the center of town. A block away one can see the imposing shell of his stone grist mill, the only one he built that is still standing.

St. Vrain's grave is on the edge of town in a small family cemetery. He died at home on October 28, 1870, having been a participant in much of New Mexico's stirring history of the 19th century.

Preface and Acknowledgments

This book was written with two related goals in mind, one historical and the other archaeological. The former derives from the latter. The archaeological goal is to provide a detailed report on excavations of Ceran St. Vrain's first flour mill, near Ranchos de Taos, New Mexico. I directed the excavation of this 1849 mill back in 1973, but never published the field and laboratory notes, which, along with the artifacts, reside at the nearby Fort Burgwin Research Center.

In my search for documentation on this mill, I became absorbed in the rich biographical data on Ceran St. Vrain and his family. He had crossed my path briefly when I was writing an article on the history and archaeology of Cantonment ("Fort") Burgwin.[1] The diverse roles he played in both military leadership alongside U.S. dragoons and in commercial transactions with the fort's quartermaster intrigued me. When I later began reviewing material for the mill report, I was struck by the few published accounts of this influential citizen-soldier and businessman.

It was at this point that I determined to discover as much personal history behind Ceran's venture into commercial flour milling as was available, and to weave this story into the archaeological account. I wound up attaching it, instead. The two parts would logically appeal to different audiences.

Part I, therefore, focuses on the life of Ceran St. Vrain. While it describes his initial career as trapper and trader in the vast beaver industry of the frontier West, its concentration is on his entrepreneurship in grain processing, principally through his flour mills in New Mexico and Colorado, and the legacy he provided for his family. There are numerous accounts here—as well as photographs—not previously published, and these should appeal to students of frontier history. There are also unfortunate gaps, because the record is so incomplete. It does not help that Ceran's notes and records were destroyed in an office fire in 1871, the year after his death.[2] I welcome any additional documentation that may be in possession of those who read this.

Part II is the report on the archaeological excavations and artifact analyses of St. Vrain's first mill. It incorporates interpretations based on not only historical accounts, but on the eyewitness recollections of two citizens who were familiar with the operation in the closing years of the 19th and initial years of the 20th centuries. When his mill burned in 1864, Ceran abandoned it and instead built another mill—this one of stone—in Mora. The Taos mill lay in ruins for some time, but was rebuilt and reused as a water-powered mill late in the century. The excavations thus reflect much more of the later operation than the former. This part should appeal to those interested in historical archaeology. Detailed information not included here is available at the Research Center for interested students and scholars to examine.

Responsibilities of director of archaeology at Fort Burgwin passed to others after 1973 and further excavations, which could have shed more light on its final years, were not conducted at the mill site. Unknowns in the history of the Taos mill therefore remain provocative.

I must acknowledge special contributions to this work by those without whom it would have been seriously incomplete. I was fortunate, at the very beginning of my research, to meet Christine St. Vrain, fourth generation great-granddaughter of Ceran's younger brother Domatille. As the informal keeper of the St. Vrain geneaology and history, Christine became a partner in my investigations and a wellspring of vital information. What she did not immediately know, she found out, either through correspondence with the large number of St. Vrain collateral descendants, or by time spent at the State Records and Archives Center in Santa Fe.

Several previously unpublished photographs of the family were kindly provided by Felicia Hall, third generation great-granddaughter of Felicitas St. Vrain Gallegos, youngest daughter of Ceran St. Vrain and Louisa Branch. Others were provided by Bob Dodson, 4th generation descendant of Benedict Marcellin St. Vrain. There were many archivists who also provided assistance, and I thank them all. In particular, Russell Martin, Director of the DeGolyer Library at Southern Methodist Univerty, kindly loaned me papers from the Janet Lecompte Collection before they were catalogued, and these proved critical to my research. Several others who provided particular information are acknowledged in the endnotes. In the introduction to Part II, I acknowledge by name the numerous students who participated in the excavations, drew the maps and profiles, and authored sections of the final field report.

It is therefore with a deep sense of gratitude to all who participated in this project that I present it here for others to enjoy.

Part I: Historical Background

When he died in 1870 at age 68, Ceran St. Vrain had lived a life filled with more adventure than most 21st century citizens could ever expect, and in a greater variety of occupations. In each of these, he not only excelled, but gained the admiration and respect of those he encountered. With energy and intelligence, Ceran met every challenge with a combination of optimism and perseverance.

In his initial adventures in the fur trade, he led hunters in treacherous terrain during freezing winters, taking charge when his mentor Sylvestre Pratte died, and paying Pratte's men and his debts with his own money. In the highly competitive commercial trade, he established partnerships and retail trade that placed him in the top ranks of successful businessmen. He was instrumental in helping settle the financial affairs of partner and New Mexico Governor Charles Bent after his assassination.

His pioneering efforts in commercial flour production led the territory—first New Mexico and then Colorado—in achieving an entrepreneurial transformation from an initial penny-capitalism. Yet his humanity spurred him to lead efforts to provide flour during times of famine and military action in struggles against both Native American and Confederate enemies.

The following chapters aim to provide brief recapitulation of this colorful half-century career in the new territories west of the Mississippi. It means to show how he developed from a young fur trade mountaineer into a highly respected entrepreneur. It is thus the flesh-and-blood counterpart to the science-and-technology of Part II.

1

Ceran St. Vrain and His New Mexico Connections

In 1849 an enterprising merchant, entrepreneur, and long-time resident of Taos, New Mexico, signed a contract with the U.S. Government to supply the army in New Mexico with one million pounds of "good, mercantable, superfine flour" over the following three years. He as yet had no mill capable of producing flour, and the dozens of small grist mills scattered among settlements in the northern valleys would have been collectively insufficient. Nor had he any experience in operating a flour mill. But wheat was grown in sufficient quantity in the region—over 70,000 bushels in a good season—and could be purchased from farmers at a sufficiently low rate to make milling a profitable business. The opportunistic Ceran St. Vrain was undaunted. Taking the longer view, he saw the almost unlimited potential for production and profit in supplying the growing U.S. Army with one of its most needed staples.

In the following year, St. Vrain began milling wheat at his newly-constructed mills in Taos and Mora, using experienced millers he hired and millstones he purchased in Westport (now Kansas City). Thus began still another venture for this prodigious citizen of the new American West, who would establish additional mills during the succeeding two decades and become one of the most prominent and successful entrepreneurs in the southwest.

The St. Vrain Family

Ceran de Hault de Lassus de St. Vrain was born at Spanish Lake, near St. Louis, Missouri, on May 5, 1802.[1] His father, Jacques Marcellin Ceran de Hault de Lassus de St. Vrain, was a French immigrant who settled near Saint Genevieve, Missouri, in the 1790s. His mother was Marie Felicité (Chauvet) Dubreuil. Ceran was one of ten children—fourth eldest—and for this and succeeding generations, the Frontier West would become home to many members of the family St. Vrain.

Ceran's father had been an officer in the French navy and his uncle, Charles, had served honorably and heroically in the French army during the French Revolution, and later as bodyguard for King Carlos III. After Charles emigrated to Louisiana, the king appointed him Lieutenant Governor of Upper Louisiana. Ceran's father, Jaques, settled in Missouri, ostensibly adding the "St. Vrain" family name to his in order to avoid confusion with his brother. Jaques met and married Marie Felicité Debreuil (*dit* Chauvet) on May 2, 1796, and established a brewery at Bellfontaine, fourteen miles north of St. Louis.

When his brewery burned in 1813, Jaques never recovered, dying penniless in 1818. With ten children to care for, four of them not yet in their teens, Marie Felicité was forced to turn to friends and relatives of good will for help. Ceran went to stay with—and work for—General Bernard Pratte, a St. Louis Merchant becoming prominent in the fur trade. That very year, 1818, Pratte had joined in a partnership with Jean Pierre Cabanné, Manuel Lisa, and others to found the Cabanné and Company.

The Pratte and Dellasus families had developed a friendship over the years, and both were typically large. Of the Prattes' seven children, the eldest two were males. The second son, Bernard Abbadie Pratte, Jr., was Ceran's age, and the eldest, Sylvestre Sebastien Pratte, was four years older. When Sylvestre was twenty-three he married Odille Delassus, Ceran's first cousin.[2]

I find no record of where Ceran's other siblings lived immediately after their father's death. The eldest, Charles Emanuel, had married four months before his father's death, and it is possible that Felix Auguste had also married. Felix lived in Kaskaskia, Illinois in 1825 and is listed in the 1830 census as operating a steam sawmill there, but it is also known that he and Charles were involved in the Indian trade enough to be well acquainted with Thomas Forsyth, another frontiersman and Indian trader. Forsyth served as a Unites States Indian Agent to the Saulk and Fox tribes in the late 1820s, and when he resigned in 1830, Felix was appointed to take his place.

Savinien also worked with brother Charles. In 1824 he went across the river to Kaskaskia, where he clerked for his older brother for a short time. He first married in 1830, and apparently spent a life of civil service in Randolf County, Illinois, serving as county treasurer in 1842 and clerk of the general and civil court in 1860.

The genealogy does not list all of the alternative names by which many of the family members were known, and it is not always clear, when family members share the same name, e.g., Felix, for whom a reference is intended. Individuals born or living in New Mexico were often identified in

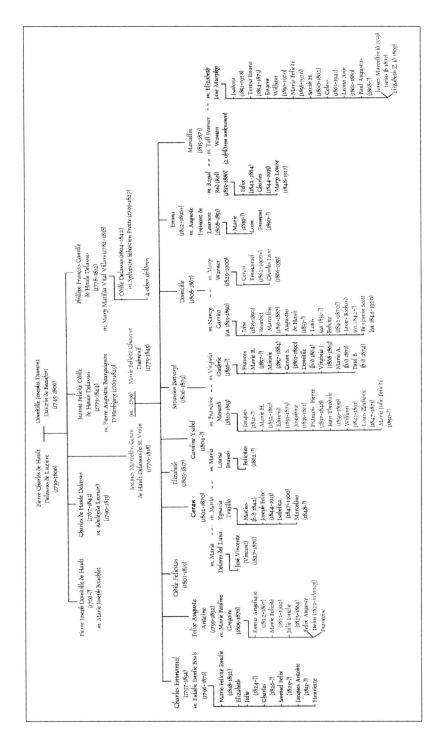

1. Geneaology of the St. Vrain family

official documents by hispanicized versions of their names when the equivalent was known, e.g., Vincent /Vicente, Marcellin/Marcellino; otherwise, phonetic equivalents were used. These can be confusing, e.g., the French "St. Vrain" becomes "Sambrano".

Adventures in the Fur Trade

With the Louisiana Purchase of 1804, when Ceran was two years old, the United States acquired the vast expanse that was to include most or all of Arkansas, Colorado, Iowa, Kansas, Louisiana, Minnesota, Missouri, Montana, Nebraska, North and South Dakota, Oklahoma, and Wyoming. The country's western frontier suddenly lurched west of the Mississippi by some 800-1,000 miles, and both the Canadian and American fur trapping and trading enterprises burgeoned. Ceran St. Vrain was eager join the pioneers. For almost two years as a young clerk in the reorganized Bernard Pratte and Company's store in St. Louis, Ceran was earning twenty dollars a month selling goods, managing inventory, and acquiring more than a passing interest in the stories told by traders returning from their western haunts.

In 1824, the energized twenty-one year old joined a handful of merchants in William Becknell's caravan, seeking profit in the New Mexican trade. In partnership with François Guerin, and with the Pratte company owning one-third of the stock, he left St. Louis in October, 1824, and trudged the Santa Fe trail with goods destined for the fur traders in Taos. On April 27th, 1824, five weeks in Taos, he wrote (in phonetic English) to his benefactor Pratte:

> After a long and trublesum voyage of five months we have at length rech [reached] this place it is now 37 days since we arrived and we have Sold but verry few goods & goods is at a verry reduced price at present, I am in hopes that when the hunters come in from there hunt that I will Sell out to Provoe & Leclere. . . . Should I succeed there is no doubt but it will [be] a verry profitable business. [4]

By July the situation had improved, in business if not in ambience. In a letter to his mother from Taos in July, 1925, Ceran wrote that "I am oblige to spend the winter in this miserable place," but he was pleased with his accomplishments and prospects. "I have Sold the greater part of my good[s at] a verry good profit if I am fortunate enough to get paid," he wrote, and he had advanced supplies to another group of Taos trappers for the season, noting that "if they make a good hunt, I will doe verey good buisness."[5] Later that year, or early in the following, Ceran married—if not by ceremony, at least by intent—Marie Delores del Luna, thus forging his destiny and committing his future to Taos. His first son, José Vicente (Vincent) was born there the following year, on May 10, 1827, and less than four years later Ceran became a Mexican citizen-perhaps as much for reasons political as emotional, as Mexican citizens were exempted from paying duty on skins.[6]

2. Ceran St. Vrain in 1860. (courtesy of Felicia Hall)

He had dissolved his partnership with Guerin in April, 1825, as he reported in his letter to Pratte, "tor reasons too teajus to mention." Guerin delivered the letter, having received $100 and two mules, with a promise to Pratte from St. Vrain to honor his debt to the company.[7] In a new partnership that summer with Paul Baillio in Taos,[8] Ceran began, more formally than before, the business of equipping fur trappers—an enterprise that others in Taos were engaged in, as trappers south of the Platte were customarily re-supplying their outfits and re-quenching their thirsts each season in Taos. He returned to Missouri in the spring of 1826, still a newlywed, to pick up further goods to supply trapping expeditions. Legendary trapper Ewing Young had done the same, and in May they traveled together back to Taos.[9] When they arrived in Taos by late July, they already had plans for an impressive trapping expedition.

That August, New Mexico Governor Antonio Narbona issued a passport "to the foreigners, S. W. Williams and Seran Sambrano [St. Vrain]" for passage with thirty-five men "to the state of Sonora for private trade".[10] Ewing Young's passport listed his Hispanicized name as Joaquin Joon. This was to be the famous Gila River Expedition, numbering over one hundred trappers under several permits. Ceran was in, and maybe headed, one of these—and all were intent on trapping rather than on trading.[11] Ceran had returned to Taos by late spring, 1827, with what success we are not informed. We also do not know what, if any, trade or merchant store St.Vrain and Baillio may have operated in Taos, but it is apparent that Ceran stayed in Taos through the end of the year, and that he was still in partnership with Baillio.

It is also apparent, throughout this decade, that Ceran was attempting to find a profitable niche in the business of the frontier. He had begun as a trader of goods for the hunters and trappers, focused on Taos, but he also became acutely aware that there was more profit to be had in leading or joining trapping expeditions rather than simply outfitting them. As did most aspiring businesses in New Mexico outside of Santa Fe, exploiting the local resources, beaver and buffalo skins, and selling them in Missouri, was less risky and required less capital in a specie-poor territory than selling Missouri imports in New Mexico. This would soon change, both with the rise of well-capitalized mercantilism (already beginning in Santa Fe) and the decline of beaver. Ceran St.Vrain's vocation would follow this change.

In the meantime, there was still money to be made in trapping and supplying trappers. So in the spring of 1827, Ceran reconnected with his old friend, Sylvestre Pratte, joining another hunting party north, returning in June.[12] In the fall of 1827, Ceran was out again, this time as Pratte's clerk, on an expedition with thirty-six trappers, including seasoned veterans Thomas L. Smith, Alexander Branch, "Old Bill" Williams, and Milton Sublette. It was to be Ceran's longest—nine months—and last hunt. It was fraught with disaster from the start: not long after their departure, Sylvestre Pratte grew ill and died shortly afterward;[13] then trapper Tom Smith got an Indian bullet in his lower leg and it had to be amputated, Smith himself performing most of the task, earning him forever after the sobriquet "Peg Leg Smith". When they returned in May, 1828, after "the most rigurus winter I have yet Experience," Ceran sold the 1,000 beaver skins, paid off the hunting party, settled accounts with the company in St. Louis, and ended his hunting career.[14]

His budding commercial career as a merchant and supplier, however, continued. Seeking fortune once more south of the border the following September, he received a passport to trade in the northern states of Mexico.[15] He was back in Missouri in the spring of 1830, seeking an additional consignment of goods to sell in New Mexico. He signed a note payable to Bernard Pratte and Co. in April, in the amount of $2,570.63, returning with the cargo to Santa Fe and paying the sixty percent import duty. He was apparently quickly successful, however, for he sent a letter to Pratte on August 4 stating that he was sending one wagon, eleven mules, one horse, "and 653 Skeins of Bever waing 961 lbs." Accompanying the shipment were Charles Bent, to whom St. Vrain had loaned a surplus wagon, Andrew Carson (Kit's brother), and Lavoise Ruel.[16] Competition was strong, however, and it was becoming difficult for independent merchants to make a living without being able to stock inventory in a forwarding house. On September 19, 1830, Ceran wrote to the company:

> ...I was the first that put goods in the Customhouse, and I opened immediately, but goods sold very slow, so slow that it was discouraging. I found that it was impossible to meet my payments if I continued retailing. I therefore thought I was best to hole saile & I have done so....[17]

A scant five months later he had apparently sold the goods for a $7,000 profit.[18] Barreiro commented on this necessity for price reduction in his 1832 *Ojeada Sobre Nuevo-México*:

> Many of the traders, in order to return to the United States in August, burn their profits, and one can purchase [goods] at a bargain. Merchandise is sold wholesale at an increase of barely 80, 90, or 100 per cent over prices in Philadelphia or St. Louis, and sometimes it is sold for only 50 percent. These senseless sales have ruined many merchants.[19]

Instead of returning to Missouri to purchase more goods, and paying export duty on the money he made in New Mexico, Ceran had shrewdly decided to travel to Taos to purchase whatever beaver skins remained after the winter and spring hunts, when pelts were thickest. There was no export tax on skins, so sending them to Missouri from Taos would only incur transportation costs.[20] To pay for the 653 skins, Ceran signed a sight draft to a R.D. Shackleford, payable to Bernard Pratte and Company, for $3,405.12.

The Bent, St. Vrain & Company

While Ceran and Charles had been friends growing up in Missouri (Charles was only four years older), and had become closer still in the mountain fur trade and within that small and tight community of foreigners in Taos, they had not yet worked together. St. Vrain's fortune was to change almost immediately. In that fateful September, as Ceran was in Taos preparing to travel back to Missouri, Charles Bent, who had earlier that year returned with the merchandise he purchased in Missouri, had also, as we know, arranged for another trip. Both of them still had inventory to sell, but it was as foolhardy to wait for all goods to sell before re-supplying as it was shortsighted to leave unsold inventory in Taos during the long round-trip to Missouri. It was in this context, then, that Ceran was approached by Charles Bent with a proposition to establish a working relationship with him. Ceran described this proposition in a letter to his employers, Pratte & Company, on January 6, 1831:

> I had made all the necessary arrangements to Start home by the 1st of this month, and Should have Started had not Mr. Chs. Bent proposed to me an arrangement which I think will be to our mutual advantage, the arrangement is this, I have bought of Mr. Chs. Bent the half of his goods, for which I have paid him Cash. I am to remain here to sell the goods, and Mr. Bent goes to St. Louis for to bring to this Country goods for him and my Self. I remit you by Mr. Charles Bent Six hundred Dollars which you will please place to my Credit. I am anxious to now the result of the Beaver I Send last fall, and would be glad you would write me by the first opportunity and let me now what amount I am owing to your hous. . . .[21]

Thus was formed what was to become a hugely successful and long-lived partnership, and the most notable mercantile company in the territory—the

Bent, St. Vrain & Company. Since their commercial enterprise would doubtless include the traffic in furs, Charles' younger brother, William, joined in the partnership. William had been involved in trapping in the northern mountain streams and would continue.

3. Charles Bent (courtesy Palace of the Governors Photo Archives, Santa Fe, New Mexico. NMHM/DCA, negative number 007004)

But Ceran was now to concentrate on his career as merchant. Later in the year 1831 the company had a store in Taos "on the south side of the plaza" managed by Charles Beaubien,[22] and shortly thereafter another store in Santa Fe.

4. William Bent (courtesy Palace of the Governors Photo Archives, Santa Fe, New Mexico. NMHM/DCA, negative number 007029)

Trading Posts North

They of course continued to provision hunters, and to carry on a strong Indian and fur trade. Indeed, as Weber has astutely noted, "the Santa Fe trade and the fur trade developed hand in hand."[23] To help further the latter, Bent, St. Vrain & Co. needed a trading post closer to Indian territory but also convenient to the Santa Fe trade. William had already constructed a log fortification on Fountain Creek (named Ft. William), near present day Pueblo, and he urged Charles to consider building a more permanent structure. Ceran supported the idea, and by 1833 they began building—out of adobe brick made on site by imported *adoberos* from Taos—what was to become the infamous Bent's Fort, on the Purgatoire River in eastern Colorado.[24] The only privately owned fort in the Southwest at the time,[25] it was to play a profound role in establishing trade and peaceful relationships with Native Americans in that part of the Southwest.

It must have been with mixed emotions that Ceran pursued peace and trade with the buffalo-hunting tribes. He had been witness to Indian hostility in previous encounters while on trapping ventures in the northern mountains. He had just recently lost his older brother, Felix, to a band of pro-Sauk warriors, on May 24, 1832, at the start of the Black Hawk War in Illinois. They had cut off his hands and feet and eaten his heart.[26] Ceran was well aware of the intense violence with which the native tribes could wreak atrocities on whites. He also understood the resentment of tribes' loss of homeland and hunting territory, and the traders' eagerness to cheat the Indians in trade by getting them drunk on "Taos Lightnin'". But Ceran also saw the humanity and kindness of the natives. Many of his friends, including William Bent and Kit Carson, had taken Indian wives. His youngest brother, Marcellin—soon to join Ceran in the Indian trade—would himself have two native wives, Sioux and Pawnee, at the same time. Captive children had almost always been treated with kindness and affection by the squaws of their captors. And brother Felix had been respected as Indian Agent by his charges. Ceran had always enjoyed good relations with the tribes with whom he had traded, and he recognized the value of this trade to both sides, so while he may have been conflicted, he was ever the realist.

Bent's Fort offered the new company a strong competitive position—beaver from the mountain men and buffalo from the Indians. Their strongest competitor was the vast American Fur Company, through its western Agent, the familiar Pratte and Company. Close on their heels was the new company formed by trapping and trading partners William Sublette and Robert Campbell, who had constructed, in 1834, a trading post they called Fort Laramie in southeastern Wyoming, near the junction of the Laramie and North Platte Rivers. Bent and St. Vrain countered with Ft. St. Vrain on the South Platte in 1837.[27]

3. Marcellin St. Vrain (courtesy Colorado Historical Society)

......It was Marcellin for whom this latter trading post got its name, although it was first known as Fort Lookout, and then variously Fort William or Fort St. Vrain, depending in part on when either young Bent or St. Vrain was in residence. Arriving on a company wagon train from St. Louis sometime in 1835, and freshly graduated from college, Marcellin was in many ways a counterpoint to his older brother. While Ceran was tall, a bit portly, and tended to be reserved and serious, Marcellin—thirteen years his junior—stood a wiry five feet six and was as light as a squaw at under 120 pounds. He was risky and had the eternal optimism of youth, seeking the frequent companionship of whiskey and the ladies—not necessarily in that order. Both brothers were affable and gregarious, reliable companions in time of need, ingenious in getting out of difficult situations.

When Marcellin arrived at Bent's Fort, the trading post farther north on the South Platte was not yet finished. Although headstrong, his demonstrable effectiveness in trade and his combined equanimity and perseverance when confronting hostile tribes soon led the company to send him north with the responsibility of managing the enterprise against competing and nearby Forts

Vasquez, Jackson, and Lupton.[28] It was not long before the American Fur Company felt the heat and Fort Jackson closed down, selling out its inventory to Bent. Not long after, the fort that Louis Vasquez and Andrew Sublette had struggled with also closed down, and by 1845 so did Fort Lupton.[29] Bent, St. Vrain & Co. were now riding the crest of the trade in the north, even though the demand for buffalo robes would soon decline as the beaver demand already had.

Still, they were at this point better off than the sedentary merchants of Santa Fe: A popular rebellion against Governor Albino Perez in 1838 had soundly routed his troops in a pitched battle on the imposing Black Mesa near San Ildefonso Pueblo, north of Santa Fe. Fleeing to Santa Fe, Perez was overtaken, decapitated, and his head paraded around the plaza. Although the rebels, and their puppet governor, Taos Pueblo member José Angel Gonzalez, were shortly deposed and order restored, merchants had been implicated as penurious partners in Albino's draconian centralist government, and had to lay low for awhile.[30] Unrest continued to be felt from Taos to Santa Fe a year later.

With the competing forts on the South Platte closed down, and the American Fur Company confining its operations to the North Platte and beyond, there was little reason to maintain Fort St. Vrain, and by the summer of 1845 it, too, had been abandoned.[31] Enabling the company to monopolize the Indian trade had taken more than impersonal business acumen; it had taken some emotional ties as well. In 1837 William Bent had taken Owl Woman, daughter of a highly esteemed Cheyenne chief, as wife, and in 1840, Marcellin had married a thirteen-year-old Sioux girl, variously called Royal Red and Rel. Their three children were born at Fort St. Vrain—including the youngest, Mary Louise, in 1846. While formally abandoned, the fort continued to be used seasonally for some years.[32]

By this date, Marcellin had also apparently taken a second wife, Tall Pawnee Woman.[33] In less than two years Marcellin would abandon his career and his family. His last visit to Fort St. Vrain was in February, 1848, from whence he returned to Bent's Fort. A month later he was on his way to St. Louis, the reason shrouded in mystery. According to E.B. Sopris, Mary's second husband, Marcellin accidentally killed an Indian at the fort and, to prevent retribution, Ceran urged him to leave the country. According to Mary, however, as she related it to F.W. Cragin, Marcellin fell ill and "was threatened with failing of the mind." On March

1, Alexander Barclay and William Bent carried the apparently sick Marcellin in a wagon to St. Louis, where it is said that brothers Charles and Ceran paid for his recovery in a sanitarium.[34] By 1850, Rel and the children had moved to Mora, under Ceran's absentee care, while Big Pawnee Woman settled just south of Bent's Fort in Pueblo.

6. Royal Red ("Rel"), sister of Chief Red Cloud and first wife of Marcellin St. Vrain (courtesy Colorado Historical Society)

About the time Marcellin married Rel, Ceran had himself taken another wife, Maria Ygnacia Trujillo, of Taos. What relationship—or living arrangements—he may have continued to have with Maria Delores is not recorded, but Taos was becoming a cozy place for the Carsons, Bents, Beaubiens and other foreigners with their local wives, most related in extended families. When George Bent died suddenly in 1840, it is said that his wife, Cruz Padilla, moved in with Ceran.[35]

7. Mary Louise St. Vrain, youngest child of Marcellin and Rel (courtesy Colorado Historical Society)

In 1842, Ceran and Maria Trujillo had a son, Matias, who died shortly after birth, but a second son, Felix, born the next year would live to become a mixed blessing for Ceran, as we shall see. Their third child, Marcelino, born in 1847, died about one year later.

The Vigil-St. Vrain Grant

The threat of U.S.—especially Texas—expansion into New Mexico following Texas' attempts to invade and annex the territory, led Mexico's President Antonio Lopez de Santa Ana and New Mexico Governor Manuel Armijo, to two acts to defend and protect this northern province: one, threatening to the Santa

Fe trade, was a Mexican edict to close all customhouses and forbid the import of U.S. goods across the border. The second, favorable for Ceran St. Vrain, was Armijo's desire to accelerate the granting of lands for settlement by citizens on the northeastern frontier.

While the fur trade was losing both its appeal and profit, the growth of commercial interest along the Santa Fe Trail in this wilderness on the northern edge of the Southwest did not go unnoticed by the ambitious Ceran St.Vrain, now in his early forties. In 1843 Ceran and Cornelio Vigil, a Prefect of Taos and former Alcalde, petitioned the New Mexico governor for a substantial tract of land near Bent's Fort and extending south close to today's New Mexico border. In early January, 1844, "for valuable services in maintaining peace with Native Americans," the Vigil-St. Vrain Grant was awarded by Governor Manuel Armijo. Later known as the Las Animas Grant, it originally covered 4,096,000 acres. Its title was later confirmed by the U.S. Government to consist of just 97,514 acres.[36] It covered the vast and rich land between the Arkansas River and the present Colorado-New Mexico border. The names of the rivers and their valleys thus captured is a blue-ribbon list of Colorado's future: Greenhorn, Huerfano, Cuchara, Purgatory. It moreover included the entire Mountain Route of the Santa Fe Trail, so critical to the eastern source of supply to Taos and the north. Just three days earlier, Charles (Carlos) Beaubien's ill-fated son, Narciso, and relative Steven Lee were awarded the Sangre de Cristo Grant, over a million acres north of Taos along the western spine of the Rockies and absorbing most of the equally rich San Luis Valley and the headwaters of the mighty Rio Grande. The Beaubien-Miranda Grant, covering the area south of the Vigil-St. Vrain Grant down just past Cimarron, had been awarded Charles Beaubien and Guadalupe Miranda, who was Secretary of State under Armijo, the year before—finally—after having been petitioned since 1841.

Thus did the Bent, St. Vrain & Co. begin to develop properties along the eastern drainage of the Rockies, as did the individual grantees themselves. This included a ranch on Ponil Creek, near Cimarron. It seems to have been growing still in 1846, as Charles wrote to Manuel Alvarez on May 31, "I shall leave on Tuesday next; Our settlement on the Pauneill, I think will go a head, this season, as there are several persons, that have meanes desposed to join us," [37] The previous day he wrote that brother George and Ceran had selected a location nearby on the Cimarron "as the most elagable place to build and farm, they call

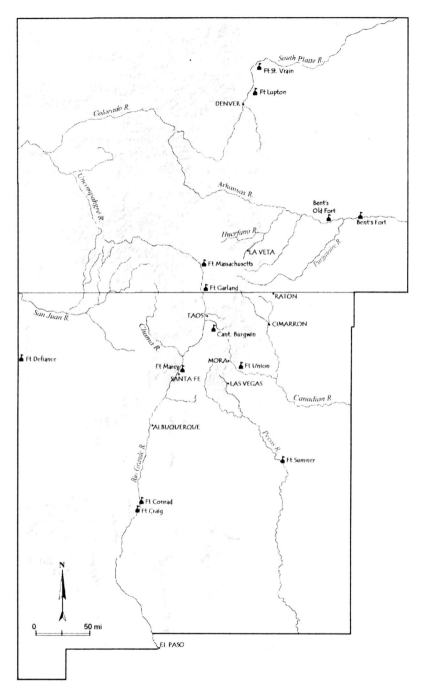

8. Map of New Mexico and Colorado, showing early military and civilian forts

this place Montezuma."[38] The firm also made an effort to reinforce their trade in buffalo hides from the plains. About 1840, they had established a small trading post on the Canadian in the Texas Panhandle—short-lived, in Comanche country and on a comanchero trail—whose adobe ruins later became known as Adobe Walls.[39]

9. Lucien Maxwell (courtesy Palace of the Governors Photo Archives, Santa Fe, New Mexico. NMHM/DCA, negative number 050592)

Still another prominent figure of the West played a central role in the eastern territorial settlements. Lucien Bonaparte Maxwell was almost larger than life and fits the image of the swarthy, self-confident frontiersman. Son of an Irishman, Hugh Maxwell, who had earned a fine reputation in business, military, and civil service, Lucien grew up in Kaskaskia, Illinois, from where so many other frontiersmen had departed for western adventure. Hugh had married Odile Menard, daughter of famed fur trapper Pierre Menard, in 1811, and Lucien was their fourth child, born in 1818. Lucien's father died of cholera in 1833, while Lucien was attending St. Mary's. He apparently stayed in school, at least for awhile, but he was already looking west. He had connections, if not credentials: Pierre Menard's sister-in-law (from his second marriage) had married Jean Pierre Chouteau, who formed the famed Missouri Fur Company, and another Menard, Françoise, had married Ceran's younger brother Savanien (who also lived in Kaskaskia).[40]

Lucien joined a Bent, St. Vrain wagon train in 1839 and wound up in the company's employ at Bent's Fort. For two years he worked at the skin trade, part of the time with Marcellin and old-timer Jim Beckwourth, who had also just joined the company at Fort St. Vrain. In Taos, in 1842, Maxwell married Carlos Beaubien's daughter, Maria de la Luz Beaubien, and in less than a week was headed back to St. Louis with filled wagons of the company train. With him traveled Kit Carson, recently kicked out of a marriage to his second native wife, a Cheyenne, accompanied by his daughter, Adaline, from first wife, Singing Wind, an Arapaho who had died a few years before.[41] Providentially, John C. Fremont was in St. Louis when they arrived, provisioning for his first scientific exploration along the western rivers. Here he hired both Kit (as scout) and Maxwell (as hunter), and both would accompany Fremont on his second and third expeditions, as well.[42]

10. Charles Beaubien
(courtesy Palace of
the Governors Photo
Archives, Santa Fe, New
Mexico. NMHM/DCA,
negative number 008799)

The Fremont expeditions both reflected and stimulated a sea change in attitudes towards the western frontier on the part of the eastern establishment: While tales of Western adventures—both on the merchants' trail and along the sinuous mountain traces of the fur trade—had captivated the vicarious imaginations of the public via reports in *Leslie's Illustrated* and in more traditional newspapers, the West was still wild and dangerous and only handfuls of emigrants had left the farmlands and towns east of the Mississippi and Missouri Rivers. Now, however, the call to realize the "manifest destiny" of the Republic was truly beckoning. The lands from New Mexico and Colorado to California and Oregon were imminently civilizable! The future belonged to pioneers who moved west to settle and stay, not trade and return! The gateway to expansion was now open—not a floodgate, mind you—but the Western movement was about to witness a small surge.

As Fremont's third expedition arrogantly transformed itself into a military effort to drive the English out of California, President Polk was sending General Zachary Taylor through Texas in another arrogant military invasion of Mexico. Both acts, half a continent away, had been contrived. It was May of 1846, and Governor Armijo had been correctly suspicious in trying to populate his territory's eastern fringe as a buffer zone against attack: On the 13th Congress declared war on Mexico, and the gathering storm approached New Mexico in the form of Colonel Stephen Watts Kearny and his Army of the West. A message to Armijo proclaimed the intent to honor Texas' claim of the territory, with the Rio Grande as its western boundary. Bent's Fort was to be the rendezvous, and by late July the troops were there.

The American Annexation and the Siege at Taos

The actual invasion had been anticlimactic: New Mexico was annexed as a U.S. Territory in a peaceful and bloodless occupation. After a brief rendezvous at Bent's Fort, the 1700 rag-tag troops marched south across Raton Pass to Las Vegas, and on August 18 entered Santa Fe, already abandoned by Mexican Governor Manuel Armijo. But the boundary claim, instrumental in placating Armijo's army by assurances that the great river would be the end of it, had been deceptive: Kearny was now encouraged to head west to California with his occupation army. The ease with which New Mexico was taken would likewise prove to be deceptive, however. Leaving a small garrison in Santa Fe, and appointing Charles Bent as first American territorial governor, Kearny and most of his remaining troops set out for California.

Thus, in the winter of 1846, St. Vrain and Bent were in Santa Fe, Ceran managing the company store, while Charles managed the fledgling government. At Bent's Fort far north on the Arkansas, their brothers, William Bent and Marcellin St. Vrain, managed affairs.

A report that some citizens of Taos were fomenting a revolt against the U.S. takeover led to Charles' decision to travel back to his Taos home and use his popularity and personal assurances to quell the pending uprising. His friends cautioned him against going without a contingent of troops, but Charles knew this would only provoke the citizens. While he had no faith in the peaceful inclinations of the notorious Padre Antonio José Martinez, who had so vehemently opposed his earlier land grant efforts, he had successfully confronted hostility in Taos before. Not this time, however. On January 18th a group of insurgents attacked various residences in Taos and Arroyo Hondo, killing and scalping Bent in his home, Prefect Cornelio Vigil, Sheriff Steven Lee, Circuit Attorney James Leal, and some twenty other officials and citizens. Included were two youths who had accompanied Bent from Santa Fe: Narciso Beabien, Carlos' son, and Pablo Jaramillo, brother of Charles Bent's wife, Ignacia. An attack at Turley's Mill, home of "Taos Lightnin'" in nearby Arroyo Hondo, killed Simeon Turley and others there, and still others lost their lives in the Mora-Las Vegas valleys.[43]

When Colonel Sterling Price heard the news in surprisingly quiet Santa Fe, he immediately sought to reinforce the protection of the capital and to gather troops to head north. Concurrently, "letters from the rebels calling upon the inhabitants of the Rio Abajo for aid, were intercepted," he reported "It was now ascertained that the enemy was approaching this city. . . ."[44] Price quickly enlisted the service of Ceran St. Vrain. One company of dragoons under the command of Captain John Burgwin, and another under Major Edmondson, were ordered up from Rio Abajo. A company of Santa Fe Volunteers was mustered under the field-commissioned Captain St. Vrain. North with Colonel Price on the morning of 23 January went three hundred forty-three men, rank and file, and four mountain howitzers. Only St. Vrain's volunteers were mounted.

11. General Sterling Price. Price is seated, center. Standing to his right is General John B. Magruder (Matthew Brady photograph, October 9, 1865. Courtesy National Archives, photo 111-B-2157)

At La Cañada (today's Velarde) they encountered some 2,000 rebels. Despite outnumbering the troops, the rebels were routed by the better weapons of the Americans. The rebels lost thirty-six dead and forty-five taken prisoners. Price lost two soldiers. The troops pursued the insurgents north toward Taos, joined by reinforcement that included Company G, First Dragoons, under Captain John Burgwin. The soldiers encountered and routed the enemy again at Embudo on the 29th. The army had taken the Apodaca route around La Mesita—the "high road" to Taos—and now, on the 30th, the troops marched towards Trampas, and the next day to Chamisal, and then across Picuris Mountain. Finally, on 1 February, writes Price, "we reached the summit of the Taos mountain," as the pass at U.S. Hill was then called, "which was covered with snow to the depth of two feet." On the 2nd they quartered "at a small village called Rio Chicito (Talpa, on the Rio Chiquito) in the entrance of the valley of Taos." This was a rigorous trek, through snow two feet in depth. Price writes: "Many of the men were frost-bitten, and all were very much jaded with the exertions necessary to travel over unbeaten roads, being marched in front of the artillery and wagons in order to brake a road through the snow."[45]

Thus, Ceran St. Vrain unknowingly passed the sites where his first flour mill would soon operate, and where Cantonment Burgwin would be erected in 1852. On February 3rd they marched through Taos to the pueblo. Here, in the assault that ended the rebellion, Captain Burgwin lost his life and Captain St. Vrain acquitted himself with such valor that he was to become a reliable and effective commander of the New Mexico Volunteers well into the following decade, leading his troops alongside dragoon companies against Apaches and Utes.

The Bent, St. Vrain & Co. partnership was dissolved when Charles Bent was assassinated. St. Vrain then briefly formed a partnership with William and his younger brother, George, to continue the business, even establishing two new stores in Santa Fe by October, 1847,[46] but the new partnership was dissolved shortly thereafter. Ceran was already losing interest in the trading business, the Indian tribes with whom they had dealt were becoming increasingly restless and hostile, and the disillusioned Ceran had offered to sell the fort to the government for $15,000, an offer which was politely declined.[47]

In that same month, October, George fell ill and died at Bent's Fort— presumably of consumption.[48] Shaken emotionally by his two brothers' deaths, William did not have the heart to continue, and presumably neither did Ceran.

In a letter to her brother Silas Bent, dated December 26, 1848, Charles' sister
Dorcas wrote:

> Mr. St. Vrain and brother William settled up the old partnership this last
> summer and settled with the Myssoury Fur Company. As well as I could
> understand from Mr. St. Vrain all the debts of the old firm were settled
> up. They still have on hand their Fort and a Debt from government I
> believe which should amount to some four thousand dollars brother
> Charles children will have their interest in that and I suppose that it is
> about all they will have after brother Charles death. St. Vrain William
> and George formed a new partnership that was also closed last year
> and William has gone out again—upon his own footing. . . . Mr. St. Vrain
> told me and I heard it from different sources that brother William as [is]
> an entirely changed man since brother George's death. . . . He says he
> intends henceforth to devote his life to his brothers children they were
> now his children and he must work for them. . . .[49]

The government debt Dorcas refers to was a $4,000 charge for provisioning
Bent's Fort in preparation for the army's failed intent to occupy it in 1837. After
long delay, the U.S. Congress agreed to pay the debt; Pres. Polk signed the bill
authorizing payment on Aug. 5, 1848.[50] William, distraught and discouraged, and
resenting the low bid that the government finally offered for the adobe fort,
burned it to the ground on August 21, 1849.[51]

It was this very year that St. Vrain, in partnership with Isaac McCarty,
added flouring to his commercial interests, bidding for a government contract
before he had a working mill or experienced millers. It was this combination of
risk-taking and foresight that characterized all of Ceran's business ventures,
and in nearly all cases his business acumen was rewarded. On the other hand,
Ceran's many contacts in the mercantile trade, and the great esteem with
which he was held in the territory, and perhaps more than both of these, his
honesty and reliability, made the transition to flour milling relatively easy for
him. In the fall of that year, Ceran was elected to be one of three Taos County
representatives to the territorial convention in Santa Fe to vote on whether
New Mexico would petition for statehood or retain territorial status (he favored
the latter).[52]

Ceran was not only astute in business, but had a reputation for being honest and loyal to friends. Lewis Garrard, a friend from 1846, admired him greatly. He "was a gentleman in the true sense of the term," wrote Garrard, "his French descent imparting an exquisite, indefinable degree of politeness, and, combined with the frankness of an ingenuous mountain man, made him an amiable fellow traveler."[53] Tall and stocky, with a round face pock-marked from a bout with smallpox acquired during the construction of Bent's Fort, Ceran earned even the respect of the Indians with whom he traded. They called him "blackbeard" from the whiskers that surrounded his face. He had a portly figure in later life when he became more sedentary.

In the 1850s he was active in helping to quell Indian depredations, participating as Captain of the New Mexico Volunteers alongside various dragoon units—many from Cantonment Burgwin, near his Taos mill. In 1861 he was appointed Colonel of the first New Mexico Cavalry, but shortly declined "on account of age" and was succeeded by Col. Christopher Carson.[54]

He began to spend more time in Mora than in Taos during the late 1860s, selling much of his property there. [55] He was smoking a cigar, in a rocking chair, at his store in Mora in late October, 1870, when he suffered a heart attack. He died on the 28th. Over two thousand attended his funeral, including Fort Union's commanding officer, Captain Irvin Gregg, and the other officers. The regimental band provided the funeral music.[56] He had joined the Bent Lodge of the Masons in 1866, and the lodge conducted the burial in the family cemetery.

Ceran St. Vrain had six children, but there is some disagreement over whether he ever married any of the three women who bore them. Christening and birth records—where they exist in mixed unions—frequently list the father as "unknown". Most of the Bents, Kit Carson, and other Anglos residing in New Mexico during this time period took wives without formally marrying them, especially when the women were Native Americans, yet they were almost always devoted to their families.[57]

All of his children were born in Taos. Jose Vincente St. Vrain, born May 10, 1827, was the first child, and apparently the only one born of Ceran's first wife, Maria Delores del Luna. The next four were born of Ceran's union with Maria Ygnacia Trujillo: Matias (born on February 17, 1842, who died in infancy); Joseph Felix (b. Nov. 4, 1843); Isabelita (a.k.a. Ysabel, b. 1844); Marcelino (b. October 10, 1847 and dying about a year later). The final union—and the only one generally accepted as a marriage by descendants—was with Maria Louisa

Branch, who bore only one child, Felicitas (b. 1862). Several of his children, as well as his siblings and extended family, will appear in the following chapters as the St. Vrain family continues to carve its niche in the frontier West.

2
Grain, Mercantilism, and the Territorial Economy

With the establishment of military posts in the territory of what is now New Mexico and portions of Colorado and Arizona in the decade following the occupation, the need to provision the troops became a top priority and a logistical challenge. The expense of freighting goods over the Santa Fe Trail was substantial. The risk of attack by plains tribes was ever present. The delay between placing an order and contracting its transportation in Missouri and receiving it at the depots in Albuquerque, Santa Fe, or Fort Union frequently created hardships for the troops. Finally, the risk of spoilage and waste in subsistence goods en route further added to the high cost and inconvenience.

During the initial occupation of New Mexico in 1846 by Col. Stephen Kearny's "Army of the West," most of the 1700 soldiers were voluntary, and individual soldiers were responsible for their own subsistence, with the exception of bread. The limited quantity of locally grown fruits and vegetables were consumed as fast as they were produced, and even the government supply of eastern flour was often supplemented by locally produced wheat flour from Taos.[1] Corn for both human and animal consumption was in greater demand, and solicitation by the army of large quantities through local contracts was made on occasion.[2]

The last of the volunteer army left the territory during the summer of 1848, leaving only three hundred regular troops. These were slowly augmented by regular army units plus a handful of re-enlisted volunteers in the years following. By the following summer the aggregate regular troops in New Mexico still numbered less than one thousand.[3]

Even before the volunteer army departed when the United States took legal possession upon the signing of the Treaty of Guadalupe, the War Department was painfully aware of the enormous costs of supplying the western posts. The great distance from Fort Leavenworth, Kansas, where military supplies were loaded onto the mule and ox trains, to Santa Fe, where the military headquarters were initially located—821 miles—added an average freighting cost of 14 ¾ cents per pound over and above the purchase price of the goods, frequently well more than the goods were worth.[4]

Much of the commissary supplies required to feed the army could not reasonably be provided by the local economy. Bacon, rice, coffee, and sugar were in greatest demand after flour and corn, and none of these were available in New Mexico, although salt was. Only bacon, however, exceeded 100,000 pounds in yearly requirement for most of the pre-Civil War period,[5] while flour, at a ration of about 400 lbs per soldier each year, exceeded this four to five times.[6]

Both wheat and corn had been important crops in New Mexico, the former introduced by the Spanish and the latter a staple since prehistoric times. Small, private grist mills were found on practically every stream in Taos Valley and elsewhere in the territory when the military occupation began. These produced flour for their owners and, through the barter economy, their neighbors.

While surplus corn was available locally to supply the army's needs, albeit with occasional scarcity,[7] adequate flour for the troops depended on both wheat production and the availability of substantial mills to grind it. The small wooden mills that dotted the streams—invariably in-stream and horizontal, or turbine, wheeled—were ill-designed for high production, each capable of grinding only a few bushels a day.[8] The enterprising capitalist, however, could foresee the great profit in local flour contracts with the army, given a reasonable capital investment in larger mills and better milling equipment.

The two entrepreneurs who first took advantage of this opportunity were Ceran St. Vrain, whose Taos and Mora mills were to monopolize the military flour supply for northern New Mexico, and Simeon Hart,[9] whose El Paso and Santa Cruz de Rosales mills would supply the southern portion of the territory. Both began their mill construction in late 1849, and in 1850 were delivering flour to the army. In addition, both St. Vrain and Hart sold corn and other commodities to the army and were involved in other business ventures.

Corn

Corn production required no processing facilities, and contracts with the army were never dominated by particular producers or middlemen. Moreover, most contracted corn was delivered directly to specific posts. For that matter, casually purchased, non-contracted corn was paid for directly by the posts themselves. St. Vrain, for example, sold corn under contract for five years exclusively to Fort Union, Cantonment Burgwin—just three miles south of his Taos mill—and Fort Massachusetts, and sold bran (a flour milling byproduct) periodically without contract.[10] In 1851, prior to the establishment of these last two posts, he supplied the sometimes understaffed garrison in Taos. In a letter to Colonel E. V. Sumner, commanding officer of the 9th Military Department, Dated October 14, 1851, he wrote:

> Citizens of this region desire one or two companies of dragoons sent here to winter. I can furnish to the troops 2,000 sacks of corn at such places in the valley where it can be furnished.[11]

12. Colonel E. V. Sumner (Matthew Brady photograph
Courtesy National Archives, photo 111-BA-1574)

As a result of the substantial demand for flour, farmers were encouraged to expand their wheat production. Corn likewise expanded to fill both military and civilian need, and there was always concern that expansion of one was at the expense of the other, particularly when drought led to crop failure. "For the purpose of supplying the mills," army inspector McCall wrote of the Mora Valley in 1850, "more wheat was planted in this valley this spring that [sic] usual, and consequently less corn, and the price of corn has therefore risen."[12] The opposite condition also existed. For example, St. Vrain wrote to E. V. Sumner on October 14, 1851, offering both corn and wheat but cautioning about supply.

> The crop of corn this season is good, but the failure of the wheat crop may have a tendency to keep up the price of corn, however I can furnish you two thousand sacks of corn and I think a much larger quantity at one dollar fifty cents a sack.
> The wheat at Abiqui [Abiquiu] and other places I will give you two dollars per fanega.[13]

On October 17, Sumner replied: "I decline [your] selling the wheat at the price you offer, but we will exchange it for corn, bushel for bushel, the corn to be delivered at Taos, or the Moro [Mora], or at both places, as most convenient to yourself." He also inquired as to the "exact measure" of a sack of corn.[14]

The following summer, however, corn was relatively scarce in the Taos Valley. In a letter to department headquarters dated May 5, 1852, Capt. W. H. Gordon, commanding the post in Taos, reported that "the citizens of Taos have said that they are unable to procure any more corn at the price stipulated by them in their written agreement. . . . We are entirely without corn and would be glad to receive instructions as to the purchase of the article."[15] In response, Gordon was directed to purchase corn from a private citizen, Juan Sanches [sic], some twenty miles south of Taos, in sufficient quantity "to give your horses and mules half forage until the time you will start to establish Fort Mass."[16]

In October 1852, St. Vrain informed the Taos commanding officer that he could supply 100 fanegas of corn (beyond that already contracted for), but no more, and the price had increased to $2.50 per fanega. The commander noted that larger quantities could be purchased in Taos for $3.00 per fanega.[17] In November, St. Vrain delivered a large supply of contracted corn to Cantonment Burgwin, and Post commander Lt. Robert Ransom notified Sumner that he had received offers in town to deliver one thousand fanegas of corn to the post in early spring of 1853 at $3.00, or at $2.50 if delivered "within five miles," e.g., at Taos or at Ranchos.[18] Sumner refused to purchase more.[19]

Forage at newly-established Fort Massachusetts was more critical, however, because of the difficulty of supplying this remote and mountainous location. Sumner withdrew most troops for the winter and assigned them temporarily to Burgwin and temporary quarters in Taos. Sumner ordered Capt. George A.H. Blake, commanding, to supply the few remaining troops and animals with flour hauled from Taos and "all the corn you can get at Red River [present day Questa] at $3 a fanega or less."[20] Blake replied, on Christmas Eve, that he would purchase all corn available at Red River, but that "they are now asking $3.50 a fanega. I have received all that Capt. St. Vrain had there, say 70 or 80 fanegas, most of which has been fed on the road."[21]

St. Vrain continued selling corn under contract to both Ft. Union and Cantonment Burgwin through 1857. In the spring of 1859, Ceran's son, Vincent, told John Kingsbury in Santa Fe that the firm had a large quantity of corn on hand, which they were preparing to sell to the Butterfield Mail Company. At that point it was going for $3.25 a fanega.[22] During the civil war years, St. Vrain had no formal corn contracts with the Army Quartermaster Department, but did negotiate with the Department Quartermaster to purchase and warehouse Taos Valley corn in 1863, when the territory's corn crop was only two-thirds of its normal yield. It was infested the following year with grasshoppers, again diminishing the yield. Quartermaster McFerran, early in 1864, sent wagons from Ft. Union to Taos to transport St. Vrain's corn.[23]

Flour

While the Army initially explored the idea of producing its own flour, and despite at least two mills constructed towards this end, in Albuquerque and in Santa Fe, it quickly gave up the idea in favor of purchasing from private sources. By the time the former mill began producing (just over 1,000 lbs. in 1850), large contracts from the private sector had already been awarded. The Santa Fe mill apparently never produced any flour while owned by the army.[24]

Ceran St. Vrain, in partnership with Isaac McCarty,[25] received the first government contract in 1849. It called for the delivery of one million pounds of flour per year for three years, beginning on July 1, 1850, and covered all military establishments in the Department except for those at San Elizario and El Paso. It was to be St. Vrain's only flour contract that called for delivery to posts beyond Taos and Mora Counties until the 1860s. It was also the largest flour quantity of any single contract with the army until 1861, although the contract allowed for a reduction or increase by 350,000 pounds in year three.[26]

Following on the heels of this, Simeon Hart received his first contract at the end of March in the following year. While quantity was not specified, he was to supply Doña Ana, San Elizario, and El Paso.[27] In 1852 new mills had been established and the army was quick to recognize the efficiency of supplying its posts from nearby establishments. Open bids were announced in March, 1853, for one year contracts, totaling 600,000 pounds. In addition to St. Vrain and Hart, who were awarded contracts for 150,000 pounds each, to supply their respective north and south ends of the territory, contracts were also awarded to Antonio Jose Otero for 250,000 pounds at his year-old mill in Peralta and delivery to nearby Albuquerque, and to Joseph Hersch for 50,000 pounds at his mill in Santa Fe.[28]

Otero had begun milling flour in 1852, and had actually first sold to the government that year under an agreement made with Sumner for delivery of 100,000 pounds at Albuquerque.[29] A well known and successful farmer and rancher with highly respected family connections, Otero had been appointed a justice of the territory's first Superior Court by Col. Stephen Kearny in 1846.[30]

When Hersch received his contract, he had just purchased his mill from John and Caroline Stein. The mill was powered by the Rio Chiquito, a small spring-fed stream which ran along what is now Water Street, eventually emptying into the Santa Fe River.[31] Hersch also sold corn to the army, and had interests in at least two sawmills in Santa Fe. One of these, sold to him by St. Vrain, had probably originally belonged to the government in the foothills where the Santa Fe River provided a powerful source of hydraulic energy. It was associated with the army's ill-fated flour mill at the same location.[32] Hersch's contribution to the military flour supply remained minor throughout the decade, although he was still active in production thereafter. In 1867, for example, he received flour contracts for Fort Bascom for 50,000 lbs and Fort Sumner for 150,000 lbs.[33]

13. Joseph Hersch (courtesy Palace of the Governors Photo Archives, Santa Fe, New Mexico. NMHM/DCA, negative number 037782)

The Economic Impact of Wheat and Corn

The increase in both wheat and corn production was an attempt to follow the growth in demand. From 1850 to 1860 the production of wheat in the territory more than doubled, from 196,516 to 434,309 bushels, while corn almost doubled, from 365,532 to 709,304 bushels.[34] This increase in demand, of course, reflects the 52% percent increase in the New Mexico population during the decade (61,547 to 93,516), accounted for primarily by military personal, a 400% increase from 885 to 3104.[35]

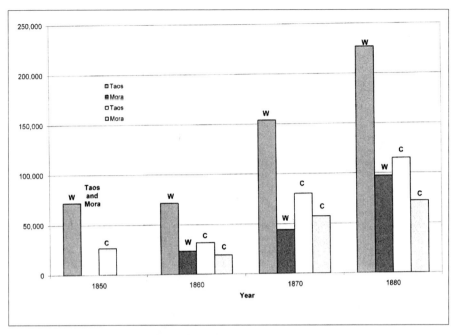

14. Grain production, Taos and Mora Counties

From the beginning, Taos Valley led the territory in wheat production (Figure 14). Aside from the predominance of Taos and Mora counties in wheat growing, the rankings for wheat and corn appear largely to reflect county boundaries, which changed dramatically from 1850 to 1860.[36] In 1850, over 72,049 bushels of wheat were grown in what was then a combined Taos and Mora County, and this expanded further in 1860 to 94,907 in the two now separate counties (Taos alone accounting for over 71,000 bushels). An observation by a traveler to Las Vegas and Mora in 1864 claimed that 60,000 bushels of wheat were grown in those valleys the previous year, noting that the calculations were "based on the quantities purchased by the merchants."[37] It is no wonder that St. Vrain's two mills in those counties supplied the lion's share of flour to the army—and it helped that the Department's supply depot, at Fort Union, was in Mora County. A distant second in 1850 was Valencia County, south of Albuquerque, at 42,983 bushels, and in third place, Rio Arriba (then listed as Rio Arribo) at 31,163. In 1860, Rio Arriba (now spelled "Ariba") was second at 44,317. All others were substantially below this.

Corn production in 1850 was dominated by Valencia County (157,795 bushels), almost three times as much as second place Rio Arriba (56,483), while all other counties produced less than 40,000 bushels. Taos and Mora had a yield of only 26,663. In 1860, these two counties together produced 50,966 bushels, increasing from 6th to 4th place among counties, with San Miguel (just south of Mora) highest at 88,492 bushels.

Colorado, 1870

Counties	Farms (ac)	Wheat (bu)	Corn (bu)	Cattle	Sheep	Butter*
Conejos	5,218	9,222	459	1,133	35,538	800
Costillo	5,583	7,420	1,650	1,267	22,510	13,430
Huerfano	2,693	5,597	13,080	2,192	30,704	0
Las Animas	1,130	5,930	2,952	257	5,202	0
Pueblo	17,087	24,451	99,380	5,483	2,166	14,963
Totals	*31,711*	*52,620*	*117,521*	*10,332*	*96,120*	*29,193*

*Pounds

Colorado, 1880

Counties	Farms (ac)	Wheat (bu)	Corn (bu)	Cattle	Sheep	Butter*
Conejos	6,279	1,607	46	2,773	25,325	3,295
Costillo	11,173	4,018	1,346	5,140	22,676	2,634
Huerfano	5,705	6,880	35,759	8,264	36,763	9,350
Las Animas	25,811	126,381	62,900	38,119	113,066	5,000
Pueblo	12,957	7,928	20,709	16,666	63,860	500
Totals	*61,925*	*146,814*	*120,760*	*70,962*	*261,690*	*20,779*

*Pounds

New Mexico, 1850

Counties	Farms (ac)	Wheat (bu)	Corn (bu)	Cattle	Sheep
Bernalillo	13,436	17,701	39,393	1,928	153,048
Rio Arriba	30,417	31,163	56,483	1,051	54,998
Santa Ana	3,197	9,740	24,373	1,741	32,035
Santa Fe	19,081	11,499	26,962	1,281	23,770
San Miguel	42,880	11,381	33,862	320	26,786
Taos & Mora	10,469	72,049	26,663	1,180	23,755
Valencia	46,721	42,983	157,795	1,684	62,899
Totals	*166,201*	*196,516*	*365,531*	*9,185*	*377,231*

Table 1. Agriculture in Colorado and New Mexico in the 19th Century

Table 1 (continued)

New Mexico, 1860

Counties	Farms (ac)	Wheat (bu)	Corn (bu)	Cattle	Sheep
Bernalillo	12,180	10,212	42,149	5,570	208,682
Doña Ana	14,490	25,293	60,636	3,397	21,637
Rio Arriba	28,077	44,317	45,538	576	14,857
Santa Ana	4,947	4,986	9,328	3,765	37,076
Santa Fe	13,266	6,061	22,913	2,560	28,910
San Miguel	21,550	9,661	88,492	2,019	96,682
Taos	9,777	71,617	31,755	3,972	96,251
Mora	3,243	23,290	19,211	2,615	36,230
Valencia	27,344	15,500	53,587	1,543	193,723
Socorro	3,175	20,965	38,997	3,812	35,368
Totals	*138,049*	*231,902*	*412,606*	*29,829*	*769,416*

New Mexico, 1870

Counties	Farms (ac)	Wheat (bu)	Corn (bu)	Cattle	Sheep	Butter*
Bernalillo	4,966	18,300	31,505	950	126,000	500
Doña Ana	17,184	23,324	11,000	20	8,774	450
Rio Arriba	6,721	5,249	10,351	1,573	40,772	0
Santa Ana	1,534	2,975	9,521	752	32,630	0
Santa Fe	10,925	6,314	20,262	630	23,843	540
San Miguel	20,541	13,321	83,145	4,571	194,309	2,242
Taos	33,686	153,799	80,224	4,104	81,108	0
Mora	90,503	44,115	57,349	4,600	30,561	4,600
Valencia	9,588	39,438	77,854	1,488	48,610	80
Socorro	4,655	26,889	26,860	1,514	23,500	0
Totals	*200,303*	*333,724*	*408,071*	*20,202*	*610,107*	*8,412*

*Pounds

New Mexico, 1880

Counties	Farms (ac)	Wheat (bu)	Corn (bu)	Cattle	Sheep	Butter*
Bernalillo	16,991	21,245	35,185	5,063	582,950	3,650
Doña Ana	46,229	62,982	41,737	3,567	34,722	2.685
Rio Arriba	61,139	53,323	42,862	16,848	147,786	8,648
Santa Fe	13,036	12,371	23,161	656	30,798	145
San Miguel	176,049	87,041	108,490	20,867	389,934	1,211
Taos	65,018	226,715	115,044	6,283	213,965	0
Mora	57,903	97,305	72,210	20,064	97,515	100
Valencia	23,225	29,852	44,304	5,851	359.325	0
Socorro	40,552	93,853	51,300	16,189	149,710	4,346
Totals	*500,142*	*684,687*	*534,294*	*96.388*	*2,006,705*	*20,785*

*Pounds

The enterprise of producing flour was obviously profitable for those who had the initial capital. In 1860, the capital investment by St. Vrain in flour milling in Taos and Mora was reported as $46,000, the total price paid for wheat was $50,000, and the labor cost of milling and delivery was $5,400, for a total expenditure of $101,400. The value of the flour produced that year was listed as $137,500, yielding a realized return on investment of 36%, a substantial economic impact on two of the poorest counties in the territory.[38] A serious drought in 1859 caused a shortage of wheat that year and the next, further increasing its price. In 1860 in Santa Fe flour was selling for $10 per one hundred pounds, and supplies had to be brought in from Missouri to feed the civilian population, according to the *Santa Fe Gazette*. [39]

St. Vrain continued to supply U.S. Army posts with flour through the beginning of the civil war in 1861, and was still selling flour at its end. He was one of seven merchants receiving flour contracts in 1861, but only he and José Otero, in Peralta, owned and operated mills.[40]

With the outbreak of the Civil war, both the demand for and price of flour increased, the latter reflecting largely transportation costs. St. Vrain's 1860 contract for delivery from his Taos mill to Fort Garland, just over sixty miles to the north, brought twelve cents per pound, compared with nine cents the previous year.[41] Competition also increased during the war years, with numerous other merchants and new mills. This led to a scarcity of both flour and the wheat necessary to produce it. During 1861-62, the Army awarded contracts for reinforced supplies at Fort Craig, on the southern portion of the Rio Grande and 225 miles south of Las Vegas,[42] in anticipation of a Confederate march to seize the Territory. St. Vrain contracted to supply both Fort Craig and Fort Marcy with flour at, respectively, 14 and 9-1/2 cents per pound.[43] Ceran struggled to meet his Fort Craig flour contract. A contract awarded on November 6, 1861, called for delivery of 75,000-100,000 pounds of flour, and in a letter of November 7 the Commander at Fort Union ordered an escort ". . . of a train of St. Vrain which will leave Mora in about six days." After delayed provisioning, the train arrived on December 22—short by 49,800 pounds.[44] In May, the commander at Ft. Craig wrote to Capt. Garrison, Chief Commissary in Santa Fe, "I have ordered 20000 rations of four to be sent from the depot in Albuquerque to this place, I have not ordered a greater quantity at present for the reason that I am in the daily expectation of the arrival of St. Vrain's train." [45] Similarly, on a January 10 order for 75,000 pounds St. Vrain delivered only 50,000 pounds, and a June 7 order for 100,000-150,000 pounds received only 40,000 pounds. Noting that the year's contracts had called for 250,000 pounds of flour, while St. Vrain had delivered only 139,000 pounds, "an absolute [deficiency] under these orders of 119,200 lbs.," the Department Commander was not pleased. He directed the Chief Commissary to

> [P]repare a statement of the damages to the United States in consequence of these breaches of contract including the estimate of damages the additional prices paid for flour & the cost of transportation when it becomes necessary to send flour from other points in either public or hired transportation.[46]

Location/ Year	Facilities	Capital Investment	Cost of Materials	Persons Employed	Cost of Labor	Value of Product
New Mexico 1860	22	$121,950	$202,100	82	$45,084	$419,250
New Mexico 1870	36	222,550	441,527	20	34,111	725,292
New Mexico 1880	21	56,550	166,390*	40	9,383	195,335
Colorado 1880	6	57,500	164,150*	16	9,880	198,290

Table 2. Cost and income valuation, flour production, New Mexico and Colorado, late 19th Century listed as value of materials. (Sources: 8th, 9th and 10th Federal Census: Manufactures)

We have no record that Ceran ever paid—or was asked to pay—damages, but neither seems likely. The government still depended on him, in his capacity of Colonel, commanding the New Mexico Volunteers, to help the territory in defense against the invading Confederates, and still needed him to supply what he could from his mills.

In 1864 Carleton got federal permission to relocate the Navajos to a new reservation at Bosque Redondo, on the Pecos River at Fort Sumner, in an ill-fated attempt to lessen the Indian threat in the west.[47] By the fall, under Kit Carson's command, some 9,000 tribal members had been marched there. St. Vrain was one of several contractors to supply the reservation with livestock, feed, flour, and other provisions. He had agreed by contract in March, 1864, to deliver 150,000 pounds of wheat meal, but the department wanted "at least three hundred and fifty thousand pounds more. . .to be delivered by installments, at the earliest practicable day, at Ft. Sumner." [48]

Date	Contract with	Wheat (bu)	Flour (lbs)	Wheat meal	Paid
28 May	St. Vrain			27,236	$2,326.02
22 July	St. Vrain		57,500	190,800	22,053.00
22 Aug	St. Vrain			10,800	918.00
23 Aug	St. Vrain			102,242	8,690.57
31 Aug	St. Vrain		2,300	1,700	374.50
21 Sep	St. Vrain			114,631	9,743.63
19 May	L.B. Maxwell	23,991			1,449.45
9 Aug	L.B. Maxwell	48,257			
15 Sep	L.B. Maxwell	35,890			
26 May	W.H. Moore & Co.			19,938	1,694.73
30 May	W.H. Moore & Co.			14,901	
13 Jun	W.H. Moore & Co.			14,000	1,190.00
31 Jul	W.H. Moore & Co.			39,394	
Jun-Jul	W.H. Moore & Co.			50,014	
28 Jul	Andres Dodd	144,757	20,500		

Table 3. Grain and flour contracts for the Navajo, 1864. (Source: Condition of the Indian Tribes: Report of the Joint Special Committee, U.S. Congress, 1865, Appendix, 273-279)

In all of his contracts that year, St. Vrain sold 59,800 pounds of flour and 447,409 pounds of wheat meal Ft. Sumner. Some 20,000 pounds of flour was also purchased by the army from "Andres Dodd"[49] in a single contract, delivered on 28 July, 1864. The government purchased over one-quarter million pounds of wheat, as well. The wheat was purchased from Lucien Maxwell (108,138 lbs.)[50] and Andrew Dold (144,757 lbs.). Even without ownership of a mill, there was ample profit to be made by buying wheat and paying to have it processed. The Dold records illustrate this:

From September 28, 1865, to February 2, 1866, he issued credit to the various farmers for a total of 2,368 fanegas of wheat. A fanega weighed 120 pounds or represented two bushels of grade "A" wheat of this date [and] was paid for at $10.00 a fanega, or $5.00 a bushel. Andres Dold could not grind his own wheat and the entries show it cost him $1.00 a fanega for grinding. Flour sold for $18.00 per one hundred pounds when he started business, and by the spring of 1866 it had gone down to $14.00 per hundred. . . . Dold could buy his wheat from the farmer, have it ground, include the freight cost from Mora and put the flour out for sale with a cost of $8.13 per hundred pounds. . .a gross profit of $9.37 per hundred, and even after the price reduction, he still made almost $8.00 on every sack of flour.[51]

After St. Vrain's death, in Mora, in 1870, Ceran's son, Felix and his nephew, Benedict Marcellin, continued the business of providing goods to the army, principally Fort Union. Felix supplied flour from the mill (see below) and Benedict contracted for corn—for example, 300,000 pounds at $1.69/hundredweight in the fall of 1872.[52]

Bread and the Quality of Flour

Throughout the military occupation, quality of New Mexican flour was a source of some contention. The earliest flour sold to the army came from gristmills operated by local farmers and merchants, the millstones were made of local rock—usually the vesicular basalt from ancient lava flows—and the flour was not bolted. Hence, reported Colonel George McCall in 1850, it was coarse and gritty.[53] McCall noted that, while the quality could never match that of flour from the east, there was in general "no complaint made by the troops as to its quality"[54] The same year that McCall made his inspection of New Mexican posts, the army convened a Board of Survey in Santa Fe, for the purpose of comparing St. Vrain's flour with that imported from the states. A loaf of bread from St. Vrain's flour was "lighter in weight" and contained "sand grit." Being unbolted, it was less porous, and thus not as digestible, but was labeled as "not bad". [55] Both McCall and, in 1853, inspector Mansfield, considered Simeon Hart's flour—produced at his mill in El Paso and at his father-in-law's mill in Santa Cruz de Rosales in Chihuahua—superior to St. Vrain's.[56] The next flour inspection, in 1869, found all New Mexican flour to be of "good quality" except for that of Joseph Hersch, Santa Fe, which was labeled "indifferent—or bad."[57]

The last comparative "bake-off" occurred in 1871 when W. H. Nash, Office Chief of the Commissary of Subsistence, Santa Fe, conducted an intriguing experiment at Fort Union. Flour had been delivered there under contract with

Vincent St. Vrain[58] and Vincente Romero[59] from their respective mills in Mora Valley. In February, 1871, a Board of Survey at Ft.Union had rejected the Romero flour. But, Nash wrote, "(W)hile I consider neither of the flour [sic] first class a careful inspection convinced me that one was little, if any, better than the other." After all, the wheat had all been grown in the Mora Valley. He had two bakers, neither connected to the post, bake bread from flour randomly selected from both sources, and found it "difficult to tell which was the better." Ingeniously, he then put Romero flour in a sack labeled "St. Vrain," and St. Vrain flour in a sack labeled "Romero," and gave them both to the post bakery. The bread baked from the Romero flour (labeled as St. Vrain) "was light, sweet," and in the Commanding Officer's opinion "the best bread he had ever seen at the Post for issue to the troops." That baked from the St. Vrain flour (labeled as Romero) "was inferior, but equal to that daily issued to troops at the post."

One of his objectives, Nash said, was "to ascertain if the Post bakers were actually using their position to strengthen the reputation of one brand of flour at the expense of another," which, it is fair to say, his experiment confirmed. All the Romero flour, he noted, "has since been consumed by the troops" He concluded that "a good baker can furnish from either brands [sic] of flour as good an article of bread as can be made from wheat growing in their territory." Cryptically, he added, "The Taos brands excepted."[60]

There were two mills operating in Taos (technically in Ranchos de Taos) at the time. For milling in Northern New Mexico in the 1870s and 80s, see Chapter 5, this volume.

Freighting Costs and Commodity Diversification

From the beginning of the military occupation, the cost of transporting goods from Missouri to New Mexico was a major source of the War Department's expenses, and it soon became apparent that contracting with civilians would be cheaper than hiring teamsters to drive military supplies on military wagons pulled by military oxen or mules. The first civilian contractor, James Brown, brought 200,000 pounds to Santa Fe at eleven and three-quarters cents per pound in 1848, compared with a cost of fourteen and three-quarters cents for government freighting.[61] By 1850 virtually all freighting was by contract. In that year, 266 government wagons freighted 580,000 pounds of supplies to Santa Fe, compared with private contractors, whose 658 wagons hauled 3,174,783 pounds.[62]

Only a few firms received subsequent contracts for transcontinental freighting to military posts, but numerous mercantile companies held occasional freighting contracts within New Mexico Territory. St. Vrain was one of these—often supplying transportation for military goods between Fort Union, Cantonment Burgwin, Taos, and Fort Massachusetts during the decade of the 1850s.

In the following decade, as his business expanded into Colorado Territory, he contracted for delivery of other merchants' goods from Taos and Mora to Denver, and between Denver, Westport, Missouri and Council Grove, Kansas Territory, and transshipping to Taos and Santa Fe. While large-scale freighting was both labor and capital intensive, in which manufacturers and sedentary merchants could ill afford the investment, small-scale freighting made good economic sense. As a flour producer and feed provider, St. Vrain found that maintaining his own wagons and draft animals was more feasible than the unpredictable hiring of local transporters, and generally cheaper than using freighters. Why not venture into small-scale freighting with these same resources? At the same time, he had begun to diversify, raising cattle and sheep at ranches along the front range in northeastern New Mexico and southeastern Colorado Territory.

The problem in freighting, of course, was "backhaul"—bringing empty wagons back from a delivery (or taking empty wagons to a supply source). This was also the case in contracting to sell cattle or sheep, when the drovers provided no income to offset the costs of their return trip.

For example, in the same year that Ceran contracted to provide wheat meal to the Navajos at Bosque Redondo, he was also taken up on his offer to deliver "one thousand head of goode sheep."[63] Presumably, both his wagons and the herders returned empty-handed. So it was highly desirable "to find raw materials to fill the empty or partially filled wagons on the light side of the load."[64] Consequently, despite a "rule of thumb" in freighting rates of one cent per pound per 100 miles (20 cents per ton-mile), wide variations, including backhaul costs, were often part of the bid.[65]

His partnership with J. M. Francisco allowed St. Vrain to utilize his wagons at the ranch in the Cucharas, south of present-day Pueblo, Colorado, to expand his services both east and south and to diversify his control of commodities to include cattle and sheep. On April 29th, 1861 he wrote from Taos that A.G. Boone[66], at Denver, "accepts our offer of eight Waggons to freight his goods from Westport to Denver, at the usual rates of freighting—as already understood."[67] This rate very likely included allowance for an empty front-end expense, because the letter indicated that the wagons would not be carrying goods to Westport.[68] He added that Marcellin (his younger brother) was going up "to Settle his business" and could help in preparing the train, but needed to return to Taos as quickly as possible "to work in the Store in the absence of Young — Mignault Who is going home to = Canada =."[69]

Butter was another commodity representative of growing diversification on the production end of mercantilism. In January, 1864, on behalf of the Francisco-St. Vrain partnership, Henry Daigre freighted six kegs of butter from the ranch to New Mexico. He carried it by wagon to Rayado, then by donkeys to Taos. He wrote to Francisco from Taos, "I have Sold two Kegs here and Sent the balance 4 Kegs to Santa Fe." The two donkeys cost three dollars each, and he reasoned that his expenses with the mule team would have cost more.[70] It is likely that butter was produced at the ranch, as butter and cheese had been produced by Pike's Peak Ranch on the Huerfano, and by J.B. Doyle & Co. on the Arkansas, since at least 1860.[71] If the former was the case, this is a rare account of local butter production during the decade. Indeed, the *Las Animas Leader*, almost ten years later, remarked on the need for local production in this terse announcement: "The man or firm who will undertake a butter ranch near Las Animas, and make butter, will become wealthy."[72]

This butter shipment was, again, a one-way delivery. Daigre was hoping to invest in a few hundred head of sheep to cover expenses for his return trip, to no avail. "So far," he wrote, "I find that all who have any Sheep, are disposed to take care of them themselves on a/c of the high Price of wool...." He held out some hope, however, of finding "someone below [e.g., Santa Fe] who are disposed to give Some on partido."[73] If the sheep were destined for the Cuchara ranch, this would have been a substantial distance for the future return of a partido share, unless the anticipated profit in both wool and mutton was felt to warrant it. We don't have records to tell us whether Daigre was successful. The ancient practice of partido was an important part of the New Mexico economy from colonial times through the late 19th century, although apparently not utilized as an economic strategy by many merchants until the 1870s.[74] The long tradition of sheep ranching in New Mexico had been declining as the Civil War began, and trailing the hardy Churro sheep to the California markets was no longer profitable. During and after the war, however, textile demand in the east and the increased wool yield of the Merino variety found a lucrative eastern market in wool.[75]

The Colorado ranch also raised cattle, primarily for sale to the army, although the competition was strong. In 1861, Ceran wrote to Francisco that "Advice from our agent in Santa Fe in regards to our beef proposal, is that our bid (10^{cts} per pound on foot) Was considered exhorbitant and not entertained." The highest bid from others was four cents.[76] In 1864, however, Mignault sold 529 head of cattle, at an average weight of 400 pounds, for $26,450, or 12 ½ cents per pound. These were sold at Los Pinos, having been driven from the Cucharas ranch, "[A]fter a very hard trip and a considerable loss on the road." The sixty to seventy head left over, "Mignault thinks he will Get leave to deliver at the Balle [valley] opposite San Elidifonso [Ildefonso]."[77]

The Rise of Mercantile Capitalism

In the 1850s and 60s, St. Vrain & Company, consisting of several partnerships, was one of the most successful of a small number of mercantile firms that had their origins in the fur trade and had operated out of Taos. Joining the old-timers Bent, St. Vrain, Charles Beaubien, and Lucien Maxwell, newcomers began establishing merchant stores on the plaza: Joseph Clothier (who married Charles Beaubien's daughter, Juana), Adolf Letcher, the brothers Solomon, Joseph and Samson Beuthner, and still later Charles Ilfeld. In the transformation from itinerant traders in the 1820s and early 1830s, to sedentary merchants in the late 1830s through the 1840s, to mercantile capitalists in the 1850s and 1860s, most of the smaller enterprises—the storekeepers and petty capitalists who bought from farmers and ranchers and sold locally and to the military—were left behind.

Predominantly due to the dependence of the military on local commodities, these entrepreneurs initially "fed at the government trough" and many became so dependent on it that they failed to survive the two inevitable threats beginning with the close of the 1850s. These were the withdrawal of troops with the advent of the Civil War, and the approach of the railroad which made eastern goods, particularly flour, available cheaply and drove the transcontinental wagon-freighting business to obsolescence.

3
St. Vrain's First Mills: Taos and Mora

When Ceran St. Vrain was awarded the first flour contract in the territory by the army in 1849, he had not yet built a mill, nor acquired any milling equipment. Furthermore, he had no experience in processing flour. He knew only that adequate wheat was already being grown in the region, and that money was to be had in the business of flouring. He was already known to the army, however, not only for his heroic leadership of the volunteers in 1847, but also for his commercial success. He had stores in Taos and Santa Fe, and had hauled supplies for the army and mail for the territory.[1] His self-confidence was as high as his self-esteem.

Ceran's store in Taos, we know, was on the plaza at San Fernando de Taos, or Taos proper. We know that somewhat later he had a store, and his flour business, at the Ranchos de Taos plaza—close to his mill—as well as a house in Arroyo Hondo. His home, however, lay behind a small courtyard fronting on the plaza at San Fernando. Here he lived with Maria Ygnacia Trujillo and their son Felix at the time of the Taos Rebellion. During the trial of the insurgents, at which Ceran served as translator, Lewis H. Garrard was invited to stay with the family as a guest. He describes Maria Ygnacia as "a dark-eyed, languidly handsome woman." Her sister, sixteen, was also part of the household.[2]

The Mill at Taos

Upon being awarded the contract, Ceran set out, in 1850, for Westport (Kansas) where he purchased five sets of French buhrs[3] and hired five experienced millers, who returned with him.[4] In October of that year, Ceran's partner, Isaac McCarty, died and the firm was dissolved. Determined to take a direct interest in commercial flour production, he moved to Ranchos de Taos, within a few miles of his projected mill. There, within the plaza, he established his home and business headquarters.[5] His Taos mill was constructed either that year or in late 1849, on the Rio Grande del Rancho just south of the Rio Chiquito (at present-day Talpa), and three miles north of the confluence of the river with the Rito de la Olla (Pot Creek). Traces of the original road are quite visible at the mill site.[6]

Deciding on the appropriate site was not difficult: at only one place was there a conveniently broad terrace immediately west of the river. Not far upstream, the river had carved out a broad valley with a braided stream, unsuitable for construction of a mill.

Furthermore, fording the river both upstream and again just north of the mill would have been relatively easy, as the stream width in both places is (and probably was, given the adjacent topography) between eight and fifteen feet. The land had been part of a community grant, the Rancho del Rio Grande Grant, awarded in 1795 to a handful of settlers at the valley's mouth, where descendants today live in the small village of Talpa.[7]

We do not know what permission, if any, Ceran acquired from the land's reputed owners, but it was not under cultivation, and the prospect of growing and selling surplus wheat would have been sufficient incentive to allow construction of a mill. We do know that land ownership was still claimed by the citizens, however. When Cantonment Burgwin was constructed, beginning in August of

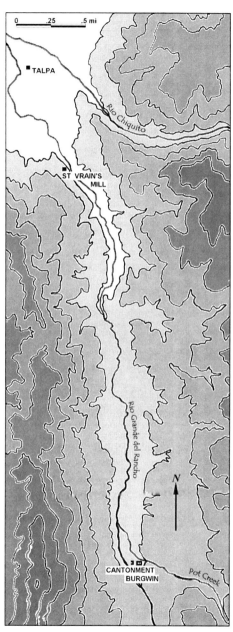

15. Location of the Taos Mill on the Rio Grande del Rancho. Map by author

1852, claimants filed suit against the army for illegal occupation. The court's decision in favor of the army rested, in part, on the defense's testimony of prior and current use of the valley by other outsiders, including "the grist mill of Capt. St. Vrain" and a sawmill "about a mile below the post," erected by Asa Estes and Robert Carey.[8] Indeed, other uses had been put to the river even earlier. In the 1830s a whiskey still was operated "about three miles up the little Rio Grande canon" by an early settler, John Rawlins, and brother.[9] In February, 1847, Lewis Garrard's party passed another distillery on this stream, just south of Ranchos where Talpa lies today.[10]

The size of his initial military contract for flour must have spurred St. Vrain to construct a second mill, in Mora, which was in operation during 1850, and under contract to purchase most of the wheat grown in that area. There is some ambiguity regarding the sequence of construction of the two mills. Lecompte claims the Mora mill was "his first and largest mill," citing recollections of Jacob Beard, his miller.[11] Frazer writes that the Taos mill was the first, erected "probably in 1849."[12] McCall's inspection trip in 1850 reported, for the post at San Fernando de Taos, "Thirty days subsistence for the present force is now on hand. Of this, the flour is made in the country." He likewise reported, from the garrison at Las Vegas, "All the wheat of this valley is already engaged by the millers at Morotown (St. Vrain and company)...."[13] While McCall fails to mention the Taos mill by direct reference, it seems certain that this mill was also in production during his visit. On January 9, 1851, the Rev. Hiram Reed, a Baptist missionary seeking a place for a mission school, visited the mill. He writes:

Today rode through the valley south of the town, and truly it is beautiful and productive beyond any other part of New Mexico that I have yet seen, Called on two Americans, who had lived in this vicinity for many years; they are wealth [sic], and will patronize the school liberally. Visited a new flouring mill, also a saw mill, objects of great interest, and sources of great wealth in this country.[14]

It may well be that both mills were placed under construction at the same time, and even probable that the construction was begun at the time of Ceran's March trip to Westport. As astute as he was, Ceran likely contracted with Taos Valley farmers for wheat as an incentive for them to plant more of it during sowing season in the following month or so. He may have done the same in Mora Valley.

Furthermore, Ceran purchased five sets of milling stones, which, according to Jacob Beard were intended for his flour mills to be built at Mora, Taos, Santa Fe, and Peralta, plus a set which he sold.[15] He obviously intended, from his initial bid for a contract, to establish a strong competitive position in the future of provisioning for the army. The two mills would serve two constituencies. The Taos mill would provide flour for the posts west of the Rockies, including Taos, Cantonment Burgwin, and Ft. Massachusetts, and the Mora mill would serve posts east of the mountains at Las Vegas, Rayado, and the important depot at Ft. Union.

The great difficulties of transporting wagons across the mountains separating Taos and Mora Valleys were well known, and would have discouraged a single large mill from serving both areas. Early reports attest to the virtual impassability of the road over the rough terrain, especially in winter. In the summer of 1850, Major William N. Grier reported that the road to Taos from east of the mountains "is impracticable, except for wagons empty or nearly so."[16] In the spring of 1852, the commanding officer of the Taos garrison reported that the arrival of a supply train from Ft. Union took fifteen days.[17] In 1853 troops under Lt. W. C. Adams redesigned the route, following orders from headquarters, "as far as my limited means would allow" making the route "perfectly open and safe for loaded wagons" and "bringing it to four days journey."[18] In January 1853, before the improvements and in snow "3 to 20 feet deep," Private James A. Bennett, with four men and fifteen pack mules, took three days to reach Fort Union from Cantonment Burgwin.[19]

Danger of Indian attack along transportation routes is still another reason to have built two mills. In the early 1850s, numerous Apache and Ute attacks and thefts were reported in the northern territorial area, especially at Rayado and Taos. In the latter place, an additional danger of insurrection also arose from time to time. On June 11, 1851, Charles Beaubien, a Territorial judge and long-time Taos resident, wrote to Governor James S. Calhoun an urgent letter concerning this dual threat and asking for immediate defense.

In connection with our entire want of confidence and absolute suspicion of the intentions of the Mexicans and Pueblos around us we have in addition the apaches Jicarillas within a few miles of D. Fernandez [Taos] some two or three hundred strong who daily obtain whiskey of the Mexicans in the ranchos or elsewhere & insult all Americans who they find alone & defenceless. The owners & operators of the mills of Messrs St. Vrain & C° in the Valley of the Rio Grande some seven miles from this place have been within a day or so past threatened with massacre by drunken Jicarrillas.[20]

The Taos mill was of frame construction on stone foundations, consisting initially of three rooms. The overshot wheel was fed by a wooden flume. The mill was supplying the posts at Taos through casual purchase in addition to departmental contract. During the construction of cantonment Burgwin, Department Commander E.V. Sumner wrote to Lt. Robert Ransom: "You will draw your flour from the mill." Two weeks later, Ransom, having expressed concern over the lack of fodder, was informed to "draw bran from St. Vrain's mill."[21]

When St. Vrain's initial three-year contract expired (as did Hart's two-year contract of 1851), Sumner advertised for additional, one-year contracts for flour. In the early winter of 1852, he asked Captain Isaac Bowen, commanding the Commissary department, to issue proposal for bids "for 1600 men to be delivered as follows, viz:

3/20 at Taos
3/20 at Fort Union
1/20 at Santa Fe
13/20 at Albuquerque
Contract for one year, reserving the right of refusing all bids...."[22]

The bids were to be opened on New Year's Day, 1853, to be awarded and signed on March 1. Sumner added specifics: "Send one of the proposals to Mr. St. Vrain at Taos, have it published in the Santa Fe papers, and have several put up at different places."[23]

The total of the awards was 600,000 pounds of flour, of which St. Vrain received 25% (150,000 lbs) for delivery at Taos and Fort Union. While the southern portion of the territory was not in the proposals issued, Joseph Hart received an identical award for delivery in the far south, near the location of later Fort Thorn. The Albuquerque award went to Judge Otero for 40% (250,000 lbs), and a 50,000 pound award went to Joseph Hersch at Santa Fe.[24]

Perhaps as early as 1851, and certainly by 1858, St. Vrain had constructed a saw mill on the property of the flour mill, although no archaeological evidence supporting this came to light during excavations. Our only evidence comes from a deed of mortgage describing the property as

> ...a tract of land about one hundred and fifty varas square situated on the south side of the Rio Grande (a branch of Taos river in said County) and adjoining and including a portion of said river with a saw and grist mill thereon standing....[25]

In 1864, St. Vrain was totally consumed with his flouring contracts. On June 29, in a letter to John Francisco in Colorado Territory, he wrote that he was so involved with his mills that he could ill afford to leave Taos to attend to his other businesses. It was inauspicious, therefore, when, exactly one month later, the Taos mill caught fire and burned, leaving only its stone foundations. The loss was estimated at $5000. In a letter to Francisco dated August 17, 1864, Theodore Mignault elaborated dispassionately:

> You have heard before this I suppose, that our old mill up here was destroyed by fire 20 days since. None of the buildings outside were burned. There was probably 40 fanegas of wheat, partly ground, when it burned distroyed [sic] in the Mill. The Mill is supposed to have Caught fire in the night at 2.00, by the Candle on the window near the Burrs, by accident while the Miller was asleep. It burned down, like Straw, in a few moments.... No local news to give you, "all well."[26]

The Taos mill was rebuilt, and continued to be occupied—although not by St. Vrain—until 1903.

The Wood and Stone Mills at Mora

The Mora mill, also of wood frame construction, was adjacent to and fed by the Mora River—probably less than a mile upstream from the large stone mill constructed by St.Vrain in 1864 or 1865. The Mora mill was managed from the beginning by Jacob Beard, whom Ceran had hired in Westport in 1850. Beard accompanied St. Vrain from Westport to Santa Fe, where St. Vrain stayed while

Beard went to Mora.[27] Ceran is listed in the 1850 census as living in Santa Fe. In his household were son, Vincente (although simultaneously enumerated in the Socorro 1850 census, as well!), Isaac McCarty, and six others, including two servants. Partner McCarty died in Santa Fe that year and Ceran returned to Taos to tend to his milling contract, possibly leaving Vincent to manage the store there. It was likely at this time that Ceran enlisted Theodore Mignault in his employ in Taos—for both the store and the mill.[28]

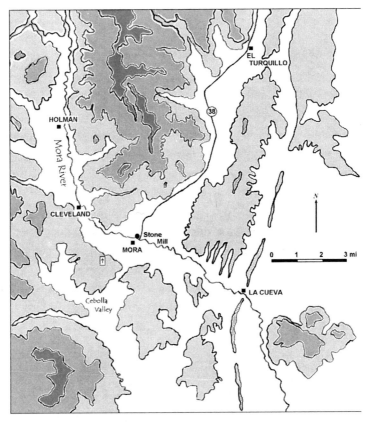

16. Location of the stone mill at Mora (Map by author)

The Mora mill was quite profitable, earning $100 a day during its first season, at the end of which Beard asked for a salary increase to $100 monthly.[29] In 1852, Lecompte continues, "Beard was replaced as manager of the mill by William Bransford, who also ran a store at Mora for St. Vrain." Bransford had earlier sold this latter property to St. Vrain and then was hired by him to manage it.[30]

In early September, 1853, William Carr Lane, Governor of New Mexico Territory, stayed overnight at Mora and commented on the mill. "Reached Mora in the rain," he wrote in his diary, "and halted at the House of Senor D. José Plai [Joseph Pley]." He continued:

> The Mora Valley is beautiful but the Seasons are too late for productive agtre. The Wheat is not yet cut & I fear the frost will catch much of the Corn. Production is greatly on the increase, & Mr St Vrain has a merchant mill here.[31]

Mansfield, in his 1853 report, and James A. Bennett, in January of that year, both note the presence of the mill.[32] When C.F. "Frank" Clarke was garrisoned at Cantonment Burgwin in 1853, he met St.Vrain, writing to his father that "Mr. St. Vrain...is now very wealthy owning & carrying on three large grist mills, several Stores and many leagues of land in different parts of the territory,..."[33] The reference to *three* flour mills at this early date is intriguingly cryptic. We know that by 1858 he owned at least three mills and later had interest in others, but there is no direct evidence, so far as I know, of any functioning third mill before this date.

He did have large holdings in Mora Valley and Taos by the late-fifties that included stores, grist mills, plus a distillery and sawmill. He mortgaged these to Joseph Pley, of Mora, in order to obtain capital for further investment in 1858, and the deed gives us insight into St. Vrain's diversified businesses.[34] Ceran owned four parcels of land in the town of Mora (then called San Gertrudas de Mora, after a land grant awarded in 1835) on both the north and south sides of the Mora River. The two largest measured three hundred *varas* (about 825 feet) in width, one fronting the main road and extending south "to the brow of the mountain which divides the said Valey of Mora from the Valey of Sevolla [Cebolla]...." [35] The second of the two extended from the river north to the mountain "and is bounded on the East by the Common land of San Getrudas...." On this parcel of land was "a dwelling house and outhouses" and Ceran's Mora grist mill. It would have been west (upstream) a quarter mile or more from his later stone mill—which is adjacent to the road to Guadalupita.[36]

It is reasonable to assume, although far from certain, that these two parcels, equal in frontage feet, faced each other from across the road. The other two parcels in town adjoined each other on the road, each only about thirty feet wide. One had a house, "formerly occupied" by Joseph Pley as a business establishment, together with a corral, and the other was St. Vrain's "mercantile establishment," sold to him earlier by William Bransford. Both parcels reached back to the Mora River.

On the road to the west of Mora just over two miles lies the present town of Cleveland, then known as San Antonio de Mora. Here Ceran owned another parcel of land "with a dwelling house with six rooms" and another store, this one occupied and run by Joseph Pley.

Rounding out St. Vrain's holdings in 1858 is a large tract in the narrow Valley of Guadalupita, some twelve miles north of Mora. Here Ceran operated another grist mill and a distillery on Coyote Creek.[37] He also owned fifty varas of land in the Cebolla Valley, probably across the pass from the land on which his family cemetery was established. To his first son, Joseph Vincent (more commonly "Vicente"), Ceran gave the responsibility of running the mercantile store and gristmill in Mora, and the distillery in Guadalupita.[38]

Despite the large holdings in Mora, Ceran had sufficient relatives and partners there to handle his business in the 1860s. There was more than enough business to keep him in Taos: He was becoming deeply involved in the merchant trade to Denver through his partnership in the San Luis Valley flour mill, his stores in Taos and Santa Fe were still competitive, and Taos was growing a third more corn and more than three times more wheat than Mora Valley.

Another wife was also in the offing. Sometime in 1860 or 1861 Ceran married Maria Luisa Branch, daughter of José de Jesus Branch (often spelled Branche) and Maria Paula Luna. She was born in Taos and baptized on May 4, 1835 at five days of age. It is remarkable that, two years earlier at her older brother Vital's baptism, the godparents are recorded as "Severiano San Bran [Ceran St. Vrain] y Ma. Ignacio Jaramillo." Maria Ignacia was Charles Bent's wife.[39] In 1859 Ceran bought twenty-five varas of land in Arroyo Hondo, including a ten-room house in the Plaza of Delores.[40]

17. Louisa Branch, Ceran's third wife (courtesy Felicia Hall)

18. Ceran's house in Mora (courtesy Palace of the Governors Photo Archives, Santa Fe, New Mexico. NMHM/DCA, negative number 9615)

Subsequent to the July, 1864 fire that destroyed his Taos mill, and burdened with large flour contracts, St. Vrain no doubt immediately began building a new mill in Mora, this one of largely undressed stone masonry with crudely-applied mortar. That year he also established a residence in Mora, but did not yet permanently move there. In Taos he had established a merchant partnership with Joseph S. Hurst in about 1863 or 1864, and Juan Santistevan, also a Taos merchant, joined them in 1865 under the firm of Santistevan, St. Vrain & Co. Then in 1867, Ceran made the move to Mora a more permanent one, spending most of his time there in the absence of a mill in Taos, and the Taos firm then became Santistevan and Hurst.[41] Ceran's wife, Luisa, and their child Felicitas, born in 1862, apparently continued to live in Taos. She is listed there in the 1870 census.

The stone mill Ceran built in 1865 still stands today, in dire need of stabilization. This mill had an elevated wood sluiceway, as did his older mill, drawing water from the Mora River. Both mills continued in operation until after his death, either through lease or sale.

19. Early photograph of Ceran's stone mill. New Mexico Department of Tourism Collection (courtesy New Mexico State Records Center and Archives, Collection 1987-066, Photo #001934)

The loss of investment and income represented by the fire put Ceran in at least a minor financial squeeze. This was exacerbated by the delay in payment for flour delivery by the U.S. Army. Exactly a month before the fire, Ceran wrote J.M. Francisco:

> I have been fortunate enough to obtain payment for the herd of cattle delivered at Los Pinos, but not so fortunate with the flour, the Commissary being out of funds—and has been since the middle of May, owing me a large amt. [42]

In December following the fire, Ceran sold the lands with mill and distillery at Guadalupita to George Gold for $4000, [43] and on September 9, 1865, he sold his land "with dwelling houses and other buildings thereon standing," in San Antonio de Mora, to James Thomas of Mora. [44] Two days later, Ceran leased the Mora property adjacent to his mercantile store for one hundred dollars per year to his son Vicente and John May, both living in Mora, and the two signed a co-partnership to "associate themselves in the art and trade of Brewing Malt and distilling Spirituous liquors" for a period of seven years. [45]

Expanding his investment in lumbering, he formed a partnership in the summer of 1866 with Theodore Mignault and John O. Smith, both of Mora, "for carrying on the manufacturing of lumber in the Turquillo [valley], near Mora...." St. Vrain and Mignault were to furnish "one steam engine of Sixteen horsepower complete, and one complete circular Sawmill", while Smith was obligated "to Construct, locate, and erect the Said engine and Mill." [46] For some unexplained reason, Mignault left the partnership that year, possibly because of his increased responsibilities as Ceran's agent in the growing flour milling and cattle enterprise in Colorado. We will discuss this more fully in the following chapter. In any event, in February, 1867, St. Vrain and Smith entered into a new partnership with Isaac N. Brister, the latter two partners having "full charge and management of the running of the Saw mill." [47]

In 1868, apparently still pressed for cash, he sold his fifty varas of land in the Cebolla Valley to Henry Jackson and his wife. [48] The following year, however, he lost the property on which his older, wood mill was probably located, when forced to sell it in payment of a debt. A sheriff's deed to the property (two parcels, each 146 by 1000 varas long, running "from the Mora River to the Northern Hills") was issued to a Delores Romero. [49] Just under a year before he died, Ceran leased an additional holding in Mora to his nephew, Benedict Marcellin. [50]

The stone mill continued in operation beyond Ceran's death, changing ownership as the years passed. The Taos and Mora mills—during the 1850s—fully established Ceran St. Vrain as the foremost contractor for flour in the northern half of the territory. Furthermore, this initial enterprise gave Ceran the experience, the entrepreneurial contacts, and the financial means to expand his business investments in the 1860s. He was thus well positioned to take advantage of the growing opportunities to the north when Colorado gold opened the gateway to a rapid expansion of settlements.

4
The Mills in Santa Fe and Colorado

Although Jacob Beard claims that St. Vrain's five sets of burrstones purchased in Westport were sent to New Mexico for use in four mills, including two in Santa Fe and Peralta, the mill he purchased in Santa Fe in 1852 had Mexican stones. The Peralta mill was first constructed and owned by William L. Skinner in 1850 or earlier, and there is no information on the source of the stones.[1]

The Santa Fe Mill

Shortly after his arrival in Santa Fe, General Kearny asked that a site for a sawmill be selected, for the purpose of milling lumber for the construction of Fort Marcy. Assistant Quartermaster Captain Thomas Swordes selected a site on the Santa Fe River in the foothills east of the city plaza and instructed that the necessary materials be sent from St. Louis. His successor, Captain W. M. D. McKissack, purchased and received title to the land on behalf of the Army for a total of $100.[2] By mid-September, 1846, McKissack wrote that he had commenced construction, but made no mention of an associated grist mill. The sawmill was in operation by April, 1847, at the "wonder and delight of the inhabitants."[3] Despite his complaint that "Corn is very scarce" and "Hay and oats are unknown," there is no record that a grist mill was planned,[4] although Assistant Quartermaster Captain S.C. Easton recalled that, upon his arrival in Santa Fe in July, 1850, the sawmill "also has a pair of mill stones for the purpose of cracking grain for animals and which makes very good corn meal."[5]

Jessup had asked Easton for an estimated value of the mill, as it was his intent to sell it. Easton remarked that he had valued it at $3500 or more when he had arrived, but that by 1852 it was worth far less. But, he added, "I do not think the mill will ever again be used by the Department as it is too remote from any point where we would likely want lumber."[6] Apparently its remoteness made flour and feed processing inefficient, as well. Flour for the Santa Fe headquarters was still contracted with private sources in the summer of 1850, so there is no good reason to believe that the Santa Fe mill made any significant contribution to grain processing for the army.[7]

In January of 1852, Joseph Hersch, a merchant in Santa Fe, acquired a grist mill and distillery on the Rio Chiquito (a tributary of the Santa Fe River along what is now Water Street), and within a few months had acquired a contract from the army for 50,000 pounds. We have no record of the original source of the millstones, nor of any flour previously produced by the mill. Hersch purchased it from John and Caroline Stein for $2377.88, and they in turn had bought it "in portions from Peter Deus and John May, Alexander W. Reynolds and Solomon J. Speigelberg [sic] at different times." The distillery had previously been operating as "the Distillery and Brewery of Deus and Company", but was under mortgage to Reynolds and May.[8] Although Peter Deus was a miller and may have sold flour casually to the army, his brother and May were both distillers, and the brewery was doubtless their primary business.

Reynolds was, in 1850, a Captain in the army and in charge of the Quartermaster Department, and became involved with the saw and grist mills erected by the army. Apparently, his chief clerk, Thomas S.J. Johnson, "owned the carriageway pertaining to the sawmill," and was paid rent on it by the army. Johnson was in debt to Ceran St. Vrain, and in March, 1852, St. Vrain brought suit against Reynolds and other parties and sought to attach the mill.[9] Reynolds was no longer in the army, but had apparently purchased property in Santa Fe and was acquiring a shady reputation for filing numerous suits to recover property.[10] St. Vrain won the suit and bought the mill at auction in June, 1852. Why the matter did not end here is not certain, but inexplicably the army was still trying to sell it during the following three months!

Then, on June 20 of the following year, 1853, in settlement of a suit against Robert Carey, Ceran St.Vrain, and Alexander Reynolds, brought by Lucien Maxwell and James Quinn, the property was again auctioned and sold to St.Vrain, the highest bidder, for $520, again transferring all right and title to the premises, "formerly known as the Reynolds and Johnson mill," by Reynolds.[11]

The land was inexplicably still in the army's hands when Mansfield inspected Ft. Marcy and the Santa Fe garrison in late August, 1853. "There is a good saw mill about one and one-half miles out of the city on the Santa Fe River and attached to it a miller's house," he wrote in his report. In an understatement, he added, "...although new..., it seems difficult to sell and a willow ...

stream ...

soldier is constantly quartered there to keep charge of it."[12] While there are no records of the actual sale, Ceran sold what was probably the machinery of this saw mill—but not the land—to Joseph Hersch a few years later, and the property subsequently passed through several owners. It is currently the Randall Davey Audubon Center, owned by the National Audubon Society.[13]

St. Vrain's Colorado Operations

St. Vrain had long been familiar with the territory of Colorado, first as a trader and trapper in the 1820s. He and the Bent brothers had constructed Bent's Fort on the Arkansas in 1833 and Fort St.Vrain in 1837 on the Platte; had made many trips across the Santa Fe Trail from Missouri with merchandise to sell at the fort, in Taos, and in Santa Fe; and in 1843 he and Cornelio Vigil had been awarded one of the largest Mexican land grants ever given—over four million acres—in southern Colorado. So by the time he began the flouring business he already had thorough knowledge the north territory and well understood its future importance. From his Taos mill he had supplied flour and corn to Fort Massachusetts in the early 1850s and had witnessed the growth of settlers and settlements along the common routes into Colorado. The rush for gold in 1858 ratcheted Ceran's business interest in the region.

There were two routes into the gold territory and Denver from New Mexico, and St. Vrain and others used them both. For the mills and mercantile establishments in the Mora and Las Vegas valleys, the easiest route was the trail north through Rayado, Cimarron, and the Raton Pass, to Trinidad—at the southern boundary of the Vigil-St.Vrain Grant—and thence to Pueblo, on the Arkansas, skirting Pikes Peak on the east, and on into Denver. Furthermore, at Trinidad, the Purgatoire could be followed northeast to La Junta and Bent's Fort and on to Missouri. This was the "Old Taos Trail," favored by traders and trappers alike, until its decline when oxen began pulling wagons across the plains and had to avoid the mountains.[14]

From the mill and mercantile houses at Taos, however, the most direct route to Colorado Territory was north through historic San Antonio (now Questa), across the San Luis Valley, skirting Pike's Peak on the west, and across the Sangre de Cristo Pass and on to Denver. Here, where communities now thrived, where markets now beckoned, and where the Taos Mountains blocked easy passage from the parallel easterly route, transportation from Taos offered direct access.

Especially noteworthy was the rich San Luis Valley, where the streams that fed the Rio Grande descended from the San Juan mountains to the west and entered the broad highland basin, fertile and already peppered with acequias.[15] Zebulon Pike had been the first English-speaking European to cross this valley, in 1807. When the Army of the West claimed New Mexico for the United States in 1846, the Spanish had already established small settlements north of Taos.

After the construction of Ft. Massachusetts in 1852, which offered protection from the Utes, settlements began in earnest in the San Luis Valley. Then, in 1858, the discovery of gold in the Pike's Peak area galvanized a rush of immigrants. While finding gold was highly unpredictable, the mining camps and villages which were quick to sprout up provided a very predictable demand for goods, including flour.

St. Vrain was quick to take advantage of the opportunity. In a letter to Josiah Webb dated November 20, 1858, John Kingsbury, in Santa Fe, wrote that the gold discovery at Pike's Peak

> ...has created no excitement here, and I think very few will go from here unless it attracts a few of the Gamblers which we shall be glad to be shed of. Col. St. Vrain is about starting a train loaded principally with Flour under charge of St. James. This is about the first benefit I can see that New Mexico has got from the discovery.[16]

Sure enough, in the spring of 1859, a new firm of St. Vrain & St. James brought "a train of six wagons, loaded with provisions and goods," including flour, to Denver. The flour was selling at $15 per 100 pounds.[17] It was freighted by James Broadwell.[18] The firm had its own warehouse and store there, "an old, long, low earth-roofed log building," but was apparently not kept for long.[19] According to William H. H. Larimer's notes, their store was on Larimer Street, "on the bluff overlooking Cherry Creek," where they "built a cabin of hewed logs which was a great improvement over any hitherto built." Theirs "was the first large stock of goods placed on our market."[20] According to William Byers in 1860, editor-in-chief of the *Rocky Mountain News*, upon their arrival St. James and St. Vrain "opened a store in the first house from Cherry Creek on the south side of Larimer Street."[21]

While the St. Vrain of the firm was Ceran, it was Edward St. Vrain, his nephew and son of younger brother Savanien (Savary), who was his agent, who made the trip with Louis St. James, and who resided a short time in Denver. Larimer implies Edward left out of fear of Indian attack. He relates an incident in which Edward was "particularly excited" over a nearby camp "up the Creek, preparing for an attack." It never happened, but, writes Larimer, "it was not long afterward that he sold out and left the country."[22] In May, the *News* again announced more shipments from Taos: "Two provision trains from Taos arrived here on the 25th, bringing 200 sacks of flour, beans, &c."[23] Edward was still in Denver in mid-September, 1859: he appears as witness in a transaction recorded in the Denver Land records on September 13. Boone apparently arrived the following spring to help manage the firm's Denver store.[24]

The San Luis Valley Mill

Rather than continuing to haul the flour from the Taos or Mora mills, St. Vrain thought it would be more expedient to have a milling operation closer to the demand, particularly since wheat was already being grown in the San Luis Valley. In 1856 Maria Jaquez owned the first flour mill in the valley, fed by the Conejos River just east of Guadalupe. The burrs were made from the abundant basalt in the region and thus produced a very coarse flour.[25] St. Vrain's only land ownership that far north was the Las Animas Grant to the east of the mountains.

However, in 1858 he acquired land in the Sangre de Cristo Grant from Joseph Pley for $1000. This San Luis land gave Ceran the opportunity to begin business there.[26] Pley, James Quinn, and Lucien Maxwell had each been given 1/3 title to the grant by Lucien's father-in-law, Charles Beaubien, in 1853, on word that the U.S. government would soon begin levying taxes on New Mexico land. St. Vrain later sold his interest to the just-removed governor of Colorado Territory, William Gilpin, the same who, as Lt. Col. Gilpin, was refused goods on credit by St. Vrain back in 1847. Gilpin acquired as much land as he could in the area, encouraged by prospects for mining wealth. When Beaubien died in the following year, his widow sold Charles' remaining half interest in the Sangre de Cristo grant to Gilpin for $15,000.[27]

Consequently, in 1859, Ceran St. Vrain and Harvey E. Easterday[28] signed a contract to build and operate a flour mill on the Culebra River, just a few miles south of newly established Fort Garland.[29] The contract established the new firm of St. Vrain and Easterday, to build "a water grist mill for the purpose of grinding corn and wheat." St. Vrain, for his part, was to provide the capital to purchase title to the site, all building materials and machinery for the mill, and funds "for the hire of hands to be employed in building and carrying on the same. . . ." Ceran also agreed to purchase the grain, presumably for the initial operation. Easterday would "superintend and manage the building and running" of the mill. All capital investment was to be repaid at the end of five years.[30]

Easterday and his wife settled in Culebra in 1859, where he built and was manager of the "San Luis Mills." He was still supplying the military as late as 1864.[31] The partners were determined to produce a finer quality flour than the coarse, unbolted product currently being processed, and they knew that locally grown wheat had the necessary quality. By the end of April, 1860, their flour was being delivered to and advertised in Denver, but flour trains were now coming into Denver from a variety of sources, including the states, and the competition was becoming stronger.

A St. Vrain and Easterday advertisement in the *Rocky Mountain News* on May 30, 1860, page five, for example, accompanied a news item on page three from the *Bugle*, in Council Bluffs, Iowa, announcing that "Pegram, Warner & Co. sent out a train of thirty wagons to Denver City on Monday last. Each wagon contained, as we understand, sixty sacks of extra superfine flour." Pegram, Warner & Co. was an old firm whose first advertisement in the Denver paper, April 18, 1860, announced that they were "Proprietors of City Mills. Flour and Feed put up expressly for the mines."[32] The same fall, Andres Dold & Company, from Las Vegas, New Mexico, arrived in Denver to start a mercantile business, including selling flour and corn.[33]

Associations and Partnerships: The Las Animas Grant

On the other side of the Sangre de Cristos from San Luis lay the series of fertile valleys defined by the Purgatoire, Huerfano, and the Cuchara Rivers, all tributaries of the Arkansas. Here the land of the vast Las Animas land grant had remained unsettled since Governor Manuel Armijo had awarded the four-million-plus acres to Cornelio Vigil and Ceran St. Vrain in 1843. A condition of the grant required that the awardees create settlements there and show an effort to fully occupy its lands. Little had been done during the decade, short of trying to keep cattle on the grasslands. And then, of course, Vigil had been murdered in the Taos Uprising of 1847. The two had previously conveyed portions of their interests in the grant, in 1844 and in 1846, and several of these interest holders had in turn sold some of their claims, and some of these were reacquired by St. Vrain. The result was the beginning of a long and complicated legal controversy, made more complex by a reduction in the total claim from over four million to 97,000 acres by an act of Congress in 1860.[34]

In the 1850s, St. Vrain reasoned that he still held significant interest in the grant, and sought help in selling off parcels for settlement. Well-traveled routes north and east passed through the land, and despite dangers of travel, there was no doubt in Ceran's mind that this was valuable land awaiting exploitation. But only failed settlements characterized the grant during the late 1840s. The 1841 Beaubien and Miranda Grant, 1,700,000 acres adjoining the Las Animas grant on the south, had not fared so badly. The Cimarron-Rayado ranching interests, so close to Fort Union, gained special protection from the U.S. military in the 1850s, which encouraged settlement.[35] St. Vrain sought a partner who could help establish a farm and expand his mercantile business on the grant. In 1853 he met Frank Clarke, a sergeant-major stationed at Cantonment Burgwin, three miles from Ceran's flour mill, and approached him. Clarke had less than a year of service left, and in December, 1853, wrote to his father that St. Vrain

...is about establishing a farm and store on the Arkansas River near Bent's Fort for the accommodation of the California Emigration and Indian trade, and has offered me a share in it on my taking the management of the whole concern and putting in some money.[36]

He did not accept the offer, however. In May he received furlough until his discharge, stayed on as Post Sutler for the summer, and returned east in the fall.

In 1855, however, St. Vrain met another officer at Burgwin, Lt. William Craig. A recent graduate of West Point, Brevet Second Lieutenant Craig was assigned to the Third Infantry, Company G. and arrived at Burgwin with his unit, on detached service, in January 1855.[37] St. Vrain saw in Craig an excellent prospect to help manage his lands in the Arkansas Valley. The opportunity to seal an agreement for Craig's future came the following year. St. Vrain was offered a commission as lieutenant colonel to lead a regiment of New Mexico Volunteers against the Apache in the Huerfano Valley. He agreed on condition that Craig be assigned his adjutant. Seeing the vast lands of the grant first-hand, Craig agreed to resign his commission and serve as partner and agent in selling land parcels, in return for receiving a parcel for himself.[38]

In addition to Clarke and Craig, a third important contact for Ceran St. Vrain in the exploitation of the Las Animas properties was also at the Cantonment. In March of 1853, John M. Francisco was awarded the sutler position at the post.[39] Francisco was to play a central role in St. Vrain's commercial efforts in Colorado. Born in Virginia in 1820, Francisco spent his late teens on the family plantation in Missouri. He briefly entered the Santa Fe trade in 1839, and established a mercantile business in Santa Fe in 1848, in which he conducted trade with the fledgling settlements north of Taos.[40] He had great interest in the northern part of the territory, trading at Taos and beyond. The sutlership at Cantonment Burgwin lasted barely three years. In June, 1856, Francisco began a long tenure as sutler at Fort Massachusetts, including the move to its new location as Fort Garland in 1858. He was reappointed to a three-year term in 1859.[41] Still under construction when Francisco arrived in 1858, Fort Garland was being built with adobe walls, and the army hired a civilian to build and operate a sawmill for its floors. Francisco contracted to provide the adobes.[42]

The next player in the future of St. Vrain's Colorado interests was Henry Daigre. Born in 1832 in Quebec, Daigre wound up at Fort Garland in the summer of 1860, driving a supply wagon from Utah accompanying relief troops for the fort. He and Francisco became friends, and Daigre was immediately hired by Francisco.[43] Francisco, Daigre, and St. Vrain were soon to become closely associated.

Francisco was accustomed to replenish his post supplies from his Santa Fe location as well as from Denver, via the Sangre de Cristo Pass. St. Vrain, in addition to selling corn and flour to both Cantonment Burgwin and Forts Massachusetts/Garland, also occasionally sold goods to the post sutlers at his store in Taos, including Francisco, frequently on credit. Ceran and Francisco thus had a relationship of mutual trust and respect.

20. John M. Francisco (courtesy Colorado Historical Society)

Milling and Farming in the Cucharas

The discovery of gold in the Colorado mountains changed the Huerfano region profoundly. Where settlements had struggled—and disappeared—in mid-decade, the rush of prospectors suddenly made the land valuable to farmers and merchants alike. Ceran, both alone and through his agent, Craig, began selling land from the already-oversold grant: William Koenig, who had settled on the grant back in 1853 along with Charles Autobees,[44] developed a farm along the Huefano in 1859, and Richens Lacey "Uncle Dick" Wooton purchased land along the Huerfano River in 1861. Joe Doyle, who had been a freighter with Wooton, purchased land there beginning in 1859, growing crops and running cattle. He had "the first general mercantile house in Colorado" in 1859, on the corner of

Ferry and Fifth Streets, and by 1863 he had a flour mill on his Huerfano ranch.[45] The successful Doyle firm—managed in Denver by Fred Salomon—continued to prosper for nine years after Doyle's death in 1864.[46]

Francisco had long envisioned starting a farm and ranch in the valley of the Cucharas, and asked St. Vrain to sell him land there. In partnership with Daigre, Francisco agreed to purchase 41,600 acres for $75,710, with $37,710 to be paid in five installments from 1866 to 1870, most likely in the form of livestock, crops, and services.[47] Although cattle and wheat would be their principal commercial crops, beans, corn, butter production and sheep would also become important, and their flour mill would add to the produce that they sold in Denver, Canon City, Colorado City, and Pueblo, in addition to Fort Union and Fort Garland.[48] Thus, Ceran and Francisco established a long and productive partnership. On May 30, 1860, the *Rocky Mountain News* carried an announcement on page three that "Francisco, Stewart & St. Vrain's large train freighted with flour for their [unreadable] in this city, arrived on Thursday last from the Mora mills, N.M."[49]

The contract for the sale of the land to Francisco and Daigre was made on September 5, 1865, and specified that the deed of conveyance would be created "within the period of one month after the full and complete payment", designated to occur on or before the last day of June, 1870. Ironically, the contract was filed and recorded on November 15, 1870, less than one month after Ceran St. Vrain died in Mora.[50]

The reduction of the grant size by Congress in 1860 reduced Francisco's portion to 1,720 acres, just 4% of the original. Since the grant had not yet been formally surveyed, there was some haste, now, to settle on it, construct the ranch, plant the crops, and build a legal claim to title. This would require concentrated and immediate effort on Francisco's part, especially considering his obligations as sutler! The solution in Francisco's mind would require two actions: First was to enlist the help of a partner in the enterprise. Having proved himself in his industry and competence, Henry Daigre was the obvious choice. Second was to implore St.Vrain for help in providing the labor and tools for construction. This, of course, was in Ceran's self-interest, for only upon settlement could Ceran begin to get a return on his loan in servicing the competitive regional markets.

In the early spring of 1862, Hiram Vasquez—in the employ of Ceran St.

Vrain—and Ceran's second son, Felix, brought a wagon and Mexican laborers to the site of the future ranch.[51] Francisco and Daigre had chosen their site at a spot where La Veta now stands, in an open meadow by the Cucharas River at an elevation of 7000 feet, 175 miles from Denver. Here, Henry Daigre and Felix St. Vrain began constructing a fort-like plaza with locally-made adobes, eventually to be 150 by 120 feet, with walls eighteen inches thick. The interior courtyard would measure 130 by 90 feet, with a well, and large zaguan doors would open to the outside on the east. Windows and doors would be interior only, creating a cloistered world which sought protection from dangers outside.[52] Daigre supervised the work on site while Francisco continued his duties as sutler, across the mountains.

When his Ft. Garland sutlership ended in November, 1862, Francisco was in need of a headquarters and way-station for the goods which Francisco & St. Vrain would be transporting. For awhile he had a store in Canon City and a house in Colorado City (today's Colorado Springs). Finally, he established a trading post and house at Pueblo. Here, he spent a good deal of his time while the La Veta enterprise was under construction.

By the summer of 1863 most of the compound for "Fort Francisco" had been completed except for that which required lumber. This, and the flour mill, were completed the following year with the hiring of sawyers—they had no sawmill—and a carpenter, Joseph Liverneau. The mill site had already been chosen, as had the point of diversion of the Cucharas River about a mile away, in their first year. The mill had an overshot wheel, with the headrace positioned so that the water would "drop from a short cliff onto the water wheel...."[53] In July of 1864, Daigre wrote to Francisco at Pueblo:

> [T]he day you left I Started two men to Sawing and I think that they will do well at It. . . . Juan Martin the man who went to Taos for a Partner returned with a Sawyer So that I will have four men Sawing now and I hope that they will get me lumber enough in time for the Mill and house. [Cornelius] Lyon will Start to Pueblo tomorrow. I hope that you will not Keep him moore [sic] than two weeks, by that time I will have lumber to make the bends [bins] for grain and frames for the doors & windows of the house, and it is work that I cannot delay very much longer. If Lyon does the Kind of work you want well, I can Send him back to you as soon as Livernois [sic] gets the Mill running.[54]

During this time, Felix was apparently assisting the head herder, Juan de Oliveira (a.k.a. John Delaware, also occasionally represented as John Delvida), but he had also helped dig the mill-and-irrigation ditch. The mill was functional by winter. On December 15, 1864, Felix wrote to the absent Daigre, "We are getting along very well with the Mill, it is grinding every day now, and it run very well."[55]

A year later, however, the mill had apparently stopped working—possibly due to ageing milling stones which could no longer be dressed. In November of 1865 Daigre wrote to Francisco: "I hope you will not dispose of your French Burrs before coming. I think it would be to our advantage to have our mill fixed here to make good Flour, which can be done with little expense."[56] The tone of this comment, added as a postscript to a longer letter, suggests that the competition for the flour markets in Denver, Fort Union, and elsewhere, combined with the increasing profitability of their cattle and sheep ranching, had put milling operations in the commercial background. Indeed, the focus of the main body of the letter is on corn sales on behalf of the Francisco & St. Vrain firm:

> Mr. T. Mignault arrived here yesterday and leaves this morning for Capt Craig's place where he expects that their mule train is now.... [H]e still offer 3 ½ cents to Freight from Capt Craig's to [Fort] Union but say's that they can get plenty of transportation at that price. He also offers us eleven (11,00) per Fanega for Corn delivered at union. We could load Six waggon's with Corn here, but I have told him that I could make no arrangements, untill I Saw you or herd [sic] from you, as you might have made Sale of wheat to be delivered, at once. I think that he will have to pay the 4.06 for freight. I leave the matter with you entirely, we have now four waggons all ready fixed and can have two moore in two or three days. We have nearly 400 Fanegas of wheat thrashed & going on all night.[57]

Ceran St. Vrain, through all of his commercial ventures in the San Luis and Arkansas Valleys, stayed in Taos, relentlessly tied to his milling and mercantile businesses there. Taos had always been his home and the hub of his enterprises, after all, despite the increasing importance of Mora and Colorado. In a letter to Francisco in June, 1864, he lamented this:

> I am now and have been so occupied with the mill and transportation of

flour from point to point that it has been impossible for me or Mignault to absent ourselves. I am in hope of being able to go to Denver about the middle of July.[58]

Problems in the Family

Another business relationship with Ceran St. Vrain began in 1861 that had personal significance in resolving a serious family problem, and the Cucharas played a central role. In fact, two fateful events coincided in that year: Ceran's son Felix arrived in Mora from St. Louis, and Hiram Velasquez arrived in Mora from Denver.

Felix, born on November 4, 1843, in Taos, was eighteen years old and subject to periods of depression, had suicidal tendencies, and was an alcoholic. His six years of schooling—at various institutions in St. Louis—had not had the maturing and intellectual effect that his father had hoped for when he sent him there in 1855.

Now Felix was back home, helping Vincent with the Mora operations, visiting his father in Taos from time to time, and—unfortunately—spending a bit too much time around their distillery in nearby Guadalupita. It would take someone more distant than family and closer in age than brother and father to provide the right influence.

Hiram Vasquez, born on August 23, 1843, was also eighteen years old, wintering in Westport with his parents, Colonel Louis Vasquez, and Narcissis Ashcroft Vasquez. The Colonel had been a trapper in the old days, compatriot with Thomas Fitzpatrick, Jim Bridger, and Jim Beckwourth, and friend of Ceran St. Vrain. Bridger's son—also named Felix—was also in Westport and was a boyhood friend of Hiram.

The fateful connections between Francisco, St. Vrain, and Hiram Vasquez begins with a letter to Francisco dated April 29, 1861. Ceran writes, "I received a letter yesterday by the military express from Mr. Boone at Denver, by which we are informed that he accepted our offer of eight wagons to freight his goods from Westport to Denver."[59] Determined to keep Hiram safe from draft into the Confederate Army, mother and father arranged for Hiram to join the Francisco & St. Vrain train's return trip, and Felix would also go, to meet his father in Denver. The boys were given the responsibility to keep the water barrels filled.

The train bound for Boone's Denver store would be travelling with another train bound for St. Vrain's stores in Mora and Santa Fe. After several altercations and delays, during which Hiram left the train at Fort Lyon and Felix Bridger later returned from Mora to join him, the two boys reached Denver and met up with Pike Vasquez and Jim Bridger.

21. Hiram "Hi" Vasquez (courtesy Colorado Historical Society)

James M. Francisco happened to be in Denver at the time as a representative of two council districts in the upper house of the territorial legislature. He met Hiram Vasquez, who was looking for work, recommended that he travel to Mora where he could surely find employment in one of St. Vrain's businesses. Ceran welcomed the son of his old friend, Louis Vasquez, and put him under Vincent's charge. According to Albright, "[t]he exhilaration and zest with which Hiram approached his appointed tasks soon captured Vincent St. Vrain's attention.... However, the attribute that most impressed his employer was his total abstinence from any alcoholic beverage." [60] Vincent and Ceran recognized the positive influence the young age-mate could have on Felix St. Vrain, and "contrived numerous tasks and errands for their joint execution." [61]

Hiram himself recalled the situation for LeRoy Hafen in 1930. "Ceran St. Vrain was a prince of a man," he said, but "[H]is son Felix could not leave booze alone. I was sent with him part of the time to try to keep him straight" [62]

It was good fortune that their companionship grew and thrived. Now, if only Felix could be removed from the temptations of the distillery. Fate now brings the story full-circle: in the following spring (1862), Francisco made his request of Ceran for men and materials to begin his construction at La Veta, Colorado. What better opportunity than to let Hiram and Felix join the train from Taos to the Cucharas Valley! Moreover, Hiram's excellent command of Spanish would be invaluable, and spending a year or so in the high mountain valley building and operating a farm and mill would be salubrious for Felix.

Unfortunately, only fairy tales end so predictably well. As fall became winter in the Cucharas, Felix St. Vrain became more and more "cantankerous" and irascible. Henry Daigre realized that another change of scenery was called for. Since he needed to send reports on the partnership's cattle business to both Francisco and St. Vrain, he decided to let Hiram and Felix be the messengers. In Taos, Ceran determined to send the two on to Mora, for Taos was awash in alcoholic temptation. Besides, he had already planned to close down the Guadalupita distillery, and Mora would thus be a safer refuge.

For several weeks there, deliveries to Fort Union, buffalo hunting, and unloading wagon trains of supplies from Westport occupied the two boys. However, it did not take long for Felix to locate and sequester some *aguardiente* from the final batch produced at Guadalupita. Vicente and Hiram found him one day in the grist mill, where he "was not only inebriated, he was crazy, blind-drunk." [63] When he recovered, Felix sunk into depression's black hole. He "ate little, spoke sparingly, and spent hours and days staring into space." [64]

Finally, Felix announced that he was going to walk to Guadalupita to visit John Riley, the watchman at the closed distillery. The tiring thirteen mile walk ended in still another disappointment. The closed distillery stood empty with not a soul in sight. Brooding over his utter loss of self-respect and convinced that his life was not only useless but a burden to others, Felix wrote a brief note and put it in his pocket, then sat down against some rocks. Holding his revolver against his chest, he pulled the trigger.

It was the following evening when, still dosed with laudanum (tincture of opium) given by the doctor, the dressed wound throbbing, flat on his back in bed, Felix became partially conscious. Surrounding him were Vicente and Hiram and his parents, Ceran and doña Maria Ignacia Trujillo, just arrived from Taos. Morose and in pain, Felix said nothing, but silently regretted still another failure. The physical wound slowly healed, but not the deeper, more profound one. Despite the vigilance of Hiram and Vicente, the determined Felix somehow found the bottle of laudanum and swallowed an overdose. Alerted shortly thereafter, Hiram and Vicente quickly mixed and administered an emetic. A third suicide attempt resulted in a deep razor cut to Felix's hand, and now, at long last, his brother's solicitude and endurance were stretched to the limit: If Felix were determined to kill himself, he would do it back in the Cucharas!

Hiram was all too willing to return to the mountain valley. Besides, the flour mill had yet to be built. So, in the early spring of 1863, Hiram and Felix returned to Fort Francisco. There they worked in good spirits for two years. In the fall of 1864, Felix acquired a flock of sheep on partido, thanks to Daigre. Felix had now fewer bouts of depression. In the following summer, the sheep population had grown and the partido debt could begin to be reduced. While Felix's demeanor had improved, his relationship with Henry Daigre had deteriorated, and the two no longer were on good terms with each other. "Privately," writes Albright, "the Frenchman told Hiram he had requested Colonel St. Vrain to make some arrangement to remove Felix from the area." [65] Indeed, when Theodore Mignault arrived on November 23rd, en route to meeting the St. Vrain mule train at William Craig's ranch, he had been informed of the problem. In his letter to Francisco the next day, Daigre wrote that Mignault "has promised me to make arrangements to move Felix away from here at once. He acknowledges the justness of our request." [66] It was shortly thereafter that Ceran purchased the Beaubois Ranch on the Huerfano Butte as a homestead for Felix, described in Felix's land claim of 1869 as

> Situate [sic] on the Huerfano River at the Rock known as "Huerfano Butte": —the lower end of said tract of land being near the crossing of said stream by the fort Union Wagon Road and extending up said stream to the bluffs....[67]

Hiram moved his family onto the Francisco Ranch at the Cucharas, began pasturing his own flock of sheep, acquired on partido from Felix, and for years thereafter Hiram and Felix led a peaceful farming life. Hiram lived at the ranch until his death in 1939.

Felix was on the Huerfano in 1870, when his father died. In his household was the carpenter, Livernois, and their housekeeper. Ten years later he had acquired a wife, Pelagrina, twelve years his junior at age 24, and they had a four-year-old son, Vicente. Then in 1900 the census records Felix, at age 50, still at the ranch, with wife Tressia St. Vrain, age 45, and what are presumably her son and daughter, despite carrying the St. Vrain surname, Francis, 15, and Vicuby, 22. [68]

Felix was still living on his property, despite the denial of his claim, as late as 1907, when Francis W. Cragin interviewed him. Felix had apparently come to terms with his demons, as we have no indication of further suicide attempts. He died on August 23, 1913 and was buried there on the Huerfano.

7
Milling and Merchants at Century's Close

When Ceran St. Vrain died on October 28, 1870, a number of his family members had already established homes in the territory. The business interests he had built had already been partnered out to this extended family, and the St. Vrain firm continued to supply corn, flour, beef, and other commodities to the army.

Son Vincent and close associate Theodore Mignault were not only designated administrators of his will and had an inheritance provided for in it, they were also already running the flouring mill in Mora. Vincent was asked, in the will, to see to the education and health of Ceran's six-year-old daughter Felicitas, although he was not designated guardian since her mother, Luisa, was still alive. To Luisa, Ceran had this reference in his will: "It is also my wish to be paid yearly to the mother of my daughter Felicitas St. Vrain as long as her good behavior three hundred dollars."[1]

22. Felicitas St. Vrain, daughter
of Ceran and Louisa Branch
(courtesy Felicia Hall)

In the 1870 Mora census, Ceran is living in a household with Vincent and Vincent's wife, Amelia, who was 25 at the time. In that same year, the Taos census lists in a single household, Luisa Branch (Ceran's wife), Felicitas, age 8, a Margarita St. Vrain, age 3, Ysabel Branch, age 21, and David Branch, age 23. A Maria St. Vrain, age 32, lived next door with Rosa Pley, both working as domestics. It is tempting to suggest that Marguerita was a second child of Ceran and Luisa, except that she is not provided for in the will.

23. Macario Gallegos (courtesy Felicia Hall)

Felicitas had already attracted attention years before she was marriageable. In a scenario reminiscent of Kit Carson's amorous gestures towards Ceran's niece Marie Felicité, one of Ceran's employees expressed interest in Felecitas. The handsome Macario Gallegos began work for him at the age of 28. According to Felicia Gallegos Hall, great granddaughter of Felicitas, her grandmother, Ramona, told the story of the romance. "He was very handsome. His eyes were blue, complexion light, and hair a light, golden-brown."

> We were told by my Grandmother Ramona, that he was from one of the wealthiest, Spanish familes, in New Mexico. He was 28 years old, when he worked for Ceran St. Vrain, at his store in Mora, NM. He had made his intentions very clear to Col. St. Vrain, that he would work for him, until Felicitas was old enough to marry him, with Col. St. Vrain's permission, of course. Col. St. Vrain told him he would have to prove himself, by being stable, loyal and worthy.[2]

Macario at least proved himself to Felicitas. When she at last came of age—years after Ceran's death—the two were married.

24. Wedding photograph of Macario Gallegos and Felicitas St.Vrain Gallegos (courtesy Palace of the Governors Photo Archives, Santa Fe, New Mexico. NMHM/DCA, negative number 151768)

Ceran's nephew Benedict Marcellin, son of his brother Domitille and wife Nancy Carrico, was also living in Mora at the time of Ceran's death. Theodore Minault partnered with him for a short time in producing and delivering flour and corn through the *St. Vrain Mercantile Company* in Mora.[3] Variously referred to as Benedict, Marcellin, and more commonly B.M. St. Vrain, he should not be confused with Ceran's younger brother, Marcellin. B.M. St. Vrain was the second son of Domitille with his first wife, Nancy Carrico. Born in 1836, he lived in Mora from at least 1862, and on his death in 1887 was buried in the family cemetery in Mora.

B.M. St Vrain and his family continued the St. Vrain merchant tradition in Mora after Ceran's death. Benedict married twice into the Longuevan family of St. Louis. His first wife was Sarah Ellen Longuevan, whom he married in Mora not long after his arrival. She bore him two children, Maud Mary Julia, born in Mora in 1867 and, the following year, Paul Domitille, born in St. Louis on August 11, 1868. Sara Ellen died of childbirth complications the next day. Benedict then married her sister, Martha Ellen, with whom he had five children. Two, twins, died shortly after birth.

25. Benedict Marcellin St. Vrain and Martha Longuevan, possibly a wedding photo (courtesy Bob Dodson)

On Ceran's death, the ownership of the stone mill in Mora passed jointly to his sons Vincent and Felix. In Felix's absence (he was living in the Huerfano Valley, Colorado), Vincent ran the business, and acquired all rights to the estate from Felix on February 22, 1872.[4] At Vincent's death in 1876, ownership passed to his wife, Amelia Rohman St. Vrain. It is not known whether the mill continued operating after this, although the St. Vrain Mercantile Company continued in operation until it was sold to Mark Daniel in 1889.[5] In any event, Amelia exchanged the mill and other Mora properties with her brother William Rohman for land he owned in Texas. In 1912 Frank Trambley purchased the mill and operated it until his death in 1922. He had operated a small mill for private use before that time.

26. St. Vrain's stone mill in Mora in the early 20th Century. Handwritten legend reads "Top floor – Mr. Frank L. Trambley owned mill from 1912–1926. On horse Manuel Romo, Sr." (Lewis Branch Photograph Collection, Image No. 33583. Courtesy New Mexico State Records Center and Archives)

The New Generation of Millers

Beginning in 1867 new mills and new millers entered the competition for supplying grain to the army. St. Vrain's production had reached its nadir in 1864, when his Ranchos mill burned, although he continued selling corn and wheat products to the army for the remainder of the decade. Indeed, in 1872, B.M. St. Vrain received a corn contract for delivery of 300,000 pounds to Ft. Union.[6] Two of the new mills were in Ranchos de Taos, operating off of the same Rio Grande del Rancho that powered St. Vrain's ill-fated mill—but downstream, most likely beyond Ranchos itself. One was owned by Frederick Mueller (Müller), the other by David Webster.[7]

Frederick Müller had come to Taos at least as early as 1861. In that small and intimate foreign community, he became friends with Charles Beaubien, then fell in love with and married Charles' daughter Theodora. The following year, Charles deeded Müller one square mile of his share of the Beaubien and

Miranda grant.[8] To help in the operation of his Taos store—his earlier partner had been Ceran St. Vrain—Charles formed the firm Beaubien & Muller. In April, 1864, following Charles death, Müller's interest in the grant was sold to Lucien Maxwell, as was that of James Clothier, husband of another Beaubien daughter, Juana, and the firm was dissolved.[9] By 1867 Müller had formed a partnership with brother-in-law Clothier and together they were operating one of the two commercial flour mills in Taos Valley. It was located near Ranchos on the Rio Grande del Rancho, if not at the location of Ceran's burned mill, then north of it.[10] In the 1870 census, the only name relating to the operation is "Frederick Müller, Miller". The mill had a sixteen-foot overshot waterwheel running its two sets of stones, and could produce 8000 pounds of flour per day, with a reported 600,000 lbs. produced for the year.[11] In a report to his superiors in September, 1868, Chief of Commissary Captain Charles McClure wrote that flour produced by "Mueller and Clothier" was superior to any other flour produced in northern New Mexico, and "even in Santa Fe for family use it brings in the market a higher price than any other home manufacture."[12]

The other mill in Taos Valley was that of David Webster. Located on the same stream, it was the smaller of the two. Its wheel was twelve feet in diameter, had only a single run of stone, and could produce 4500 lbs. per day. Its 1870 production was reported as 400,000 pounds.[13] Webster apparently came to Taos in 1861. Originally from New York, he is listed in the 1870 census as a merchant. He does not appear in the 1860 census, but in 1861 he purchased a house and lot on the Taos plaza from George Gold, and the following year acquired two adjacent lots, one with a two-story house, on the plaza at Ranchos.[14] Captain William Nash, who succeeded McClure as Chief Commissary Officer, judged Webster's flour to be equal in quality to Muller's in 1868.[15]

In Mora, several mills, both commercial and for private processing, were present in 1870 and thereafter. The stone mill of St. Vrain is apparently the only one that pre-dated 1870. The Romero mill at La Cueva acquired greater significance in providing flour for the local population than in military contracts. Trinidad Romero and his brothers had established a successful freighting firm in the 1850s, and had provided flour on contract to Fort Union in 1867 but did not grind it. The La Cueva mill was built in 1870 with an initial capital investment of $20,000, and its two pairs of stone provided corn, oats, and wheat for private grain owners and under occasional contract to Fort Union.[16]

William Kroenig, in partnership with freighter W. H. Moore, established a grist mill at his ranch at LaJunta (now Watrous), probably in 1870. This was the old Barclay's Fort, built by Sam Watrous and, after his death, sold to Kroenig by Joe Doyle in 1855.[17] The mill had a 100 bushel per day capacity and produced 18,000 bushels of flour and 600 bushels of corn in 1870, but had only a single set of buhrs. Its 12 foot wheel was four and a half feet in width.[18] Moore and Kroenig both had long experience buying and selling food supplies and both were well-known to the military for their reliability.

As sutler to Fort Union in 1861, Moore received a contract to deliver 100 tons of hay there; the following year the army bought corn from Kroenig's Colorado ranch on the Huerfano and "accepted William H. Moore's bid to deliver one million pounds of corn from the United States."[19] After the mill's construction, Kroenig had corn and oats contracts with Fort Union in 1871,[20] but apparently no further dealings with the government. Likewise, W.H. Moore had flour freighting contracts with Forts Bayard, Cummings, Stanton, and Selden in 1867,[21] but nothing after the partnership. Despite the mill's high production, therefore, it would seem that their only sales were on the civilian market. Like the other mills in this valley, it got power off of the Mora River.

Richard Delaney's mill apparently had no commercial contracts, but is listed as having custom ground 25,000 bushels in the 1870 census, compared with 20,000 for St. Vrain and 30,000 for Romero. This was custom processing of both wheat flour and corn meal, with a total value of just over $45,000.

Like Kroenig, John and Andres Dold were well-respected merchants in New Mexico. Their mercantile stores in Las Vegas were efficient and profitable. The Dold's success in contracting to sell flour by purchasing the wheat and having it ground at St. Vrain's mill in Mora has already been discussed. The experiment in flour milling by Andres in 1870 is thus not surprising, and reflects the increased market demand for flour by the public. It also indicates the profit differential between having wheat ground and grinding it yourself: In that year, custom processing yielded Dold $8900 from milling 2500 bushels of wheat into flour, shorts, and bran for the owners. Wheat ground "for personal venture" yielded $23,618 from milling 15,700 bushels of flour valued at $17,500, presumably Dold's actual purchase cost. Thus, the net profit from purchasing, milling, and selling the product was $6118—almost $3000 less than the custom contracts.

Neither the Müller & Clothier nor the Webster mills were in operation by the close of the decade. In 1879 wealthy merchant Alexander Gusdorf constructed a large steam-powered mill on the Ranchos de Taos plaza. With a sixteen-foot wheel, the imposing three-story structure on the southwest side of the plaza clearly overshadowed the famous St. Francis of Assisi Church close by. The mill burned in 1895 and Gusdorf opened a successful merchandise store on the Taos plaza.[22]

The increase in both wheat growing and flour milling in the 1870s and beyond kept these new millers employed. The market, however, was no longer primarily the military, which had originally stimulated the milling industry in the West and kept it profitable for two decades. The railroad made eastern flour available more reliably and cheaply. The new market was the growing population of the territory, and the consequent increased demand for bread and feed. Together with this population influx came new and less expensive technologies to make milling more efficient and its products higher in quality. Steam mills became more common, forged iron replaced almost all wooden operating parts, and steel roller mills replaced the old millstones. The industry that Ceran St. Vrain introduced in 1849 would be largely unrecognizable by century's end.

Part II: Archaeology of the Taos Mill

In July of 1973 I had the good fortune to direct the archaeological field school for Southern Methodist University at the Fort Burgwin Research Center at Taos, New Mexico. The principal excavation that summer was the flour mill established by Ceran St. Vrain in 1849 on the Rio Grande del Rancho three miles north the historic fort and just inside the boundary of the Carson National Forest.

During the intense three-week field and laboratory program, twelve architectural structures of the mill were systematically exposed, along with trenches designed to locate the various associated water features. In the course of these field operations 1,545 artifacts were recovered, and these were subsequently cleaned, identified, and catalogued in the laboratory at the Center.

The thirty-seven students in the school were assembled in four teams for field assignments, and groups of 2-4 were given responsibilities for writing the thirteen sections of the final report. The superb quality of work of these students, and the accurate and precise details in both their daily field records and their final reports, has left little more than minor editing for me in preparing this publication, for which I am sincerely grateful. In the list of names which follow are several who have subsequently distinguished themselves in their professions, including archaeology. I am proud to have played a small part in their professional training.

I wish also to express gratitude to the Carson National Forest for permission to excavate this important site.

Participants in the Excavations, July 1973 were: Glenda Barber, Gregory Cross, Vicky Danforth, Marsha Dekan, Sara Dorsey, Jeanne Fillmore, Alexis Fitzhugh, Jacquiline Foote, Connie Gordon, Martin Hall, Nancy Hines, Vanessa Hunter, Mike Karpinko, William Kee, Laura Kersten, Jean Landrum, Leeds Levy, Sharron Mahone, Oliver McCrary, Marlene Meier, Charlotte Nettleton, Todd Pearson, Bert Rader, Mary Love Sanders, Susan Saunders, Dan Schores,

Nene Sims, Evelyn Sneed, Randy Stice, Sara Swafford, Jane Thomas, Benjamin Underwood, Winifred Vass, Joe Watkins, Michael Wendorf, and Melodie Zirblie. Field Assistants were Paul Larsen and Herb Mosca.

I have no good excuse for waiting so many years before publishing the excavation report. Nevertheless, in 2005 I finally committed myself to completing this work, spent the summer of 2006 re-analyzing and photographing the artifacts, and subsequent years conducting further research and writing.

It is to the credit of detailed field notes and drawings by the students, and excellent written summaries, that this report is possible. My insistent demands for accuracy in the field and laboratory at least bore some fruit. I hope the following pages reflect well on these young students' efforts.

6
The Technology of Milling in the 19th Century

Hold back your hand from the mill, you rinding girls, even if the cock crow heralds the dawn, sleep on. For Demeter has imposed the labour of your hands on the nymphs, who leaping down upon the topmost part of the wheel, rotate the axle; with encircling cogs it turns the hollow weight of the Nisyrian millstones. If we learn to feast toil-free on the fruits of the earth we will taste again the golden age.[1]

The Greeks were using water-wheels to drive grist mills at least in the third century BCE. The quote above, from Antipater of Thessalonica in the first century BCE identifies the favored stone source from the volcanic island of Nisyros. Mill technology advanced greatly in Europe before being brought to America in the 18th century, yet primitive low-technology grist mills for personal use continued to be built and used well into the 20th century both in America and abroad.

Until the U.S. military dominated our southwestern frontier, the grinding of wheat into flour for baking was done—as it had been since the Spanish introduced the grain—by small in-stream grist mills, whose coarse stones were turned by the direct action of the stream on the horizontal, or turbine, water wheels (Figure 27). Inefficient for large-scale production and not capable of producing fine-quality flour, these small mills were scattered along almost every stream with a flow capable of turning the mill wheel.

These mills were easily constructed and simple to operate, and utilized native stone. Grinding only four to five bushels per day, the mill's owners provided flour for *vecinos* living around the many small villages, or *plazas*, in Spanish New Mexico. If they grew their own wheat—as did Severino Martinez, for example—they would barter it for other products or for labor. In his Lower Ranchitos *hacienda* Severino maintained a granary room for storing corn, wheat, and vegetables for sale or exchange.[2] Mill owners who grew no wheat would grind wheat for others for a portion of the flour or corn meal.

27. Early drawing of a private grist mill (courtesy New Mexico Historical Review)

When St. Vrain and others decided to produce flour for the military, they drew upon experienced millers and mill-wrights from the east for the construction, design, and materials for their grist mills. Ohio and Pennsylvania granite millstones, or imported French *buhrs*, were used in preference to the traditional Mexican millstones, frequently made of softer sandstone or of the more durable but coarser basalt.

These larger hydraulic mills all differed in at least two additional critical features from the smaller grist mills: Their wheels were vertical, and they had gears to regulate grinding power. Many later mills had additional features, like bolters for grading and purifying the flour, and a very few were steam driven, but they were otherwise the same, and the buildings that housed them had common architectural features. By the time roller mills were introduced to replace the stones, the initial era of flour milling for the military had passed.

What we were confronted with in the archaeological appraisal of the Ranchos mill, then, could be duplicated at any of the other commercial mill sites of the mid-century from the Ohio and Mississippi Valleys west. While the architectural features were largely gone, the bits and scraps of machine parts and construction materials lay scattered amid the buried debris of a once lively business, providing us opportunities for interpreting form and function. In addition, the domestic debris of broken bottles, china, buttons, shoe leather, and other piecemeal exhibits of personal lives told us something about the timing of each occupational horizon at the multi-use site.

What is provided in this chapter is a generic account and depiction of the typical mill on the western frontier in the middle and late 19th century. Aided by the limited available archaeology of contemporary mills,[3] the investigations reported herein give a most-likely account of the long history of this complex site.

The Typical Mill and Its Working Parts

The basic components of the typical commercial frontier mill of the mid-19th century are illustrated here (Figures 28, 29), with lower case letters referencing labels in the two illustrations. With few exceptions, the metal parts are forged iron, machined in the east and transported across the Santa Fe Trail, as were the millstones themselves. Wood supporting framework would have been constructed locally, using the millwright's expertise. The primary functional requirement for a vertical waterwheel—whether undershot, overshot, or breast shot—is to transfer power from the horizontal axis of rotation to a vertical axis for grinding with minimal loss of efficiency.

As the waterwheel **(r)** turns from the fall of water flowing down the flume **(q)**, the horizontal wheel shaft that is driven by the wheel at its hub likewise turns. Held by strong shaft braces as it passes into the mill pit, or wheel room, the shaft turns an attached pit wheel **(n)**, parallel to but smaller in diameter than the waterwheel itself. This shaft would typically be made of hardwood, as it is subject to very little wear and, if well braced, little gravitational stress. The braces **(t)** would normally be iron bolted to a wood support **(u)** on the interior, but to a stone or concrete pillar **(v)** on the far side of the wheel pit **(s)**.

While both the waterwheel and the pit wheel could be wood or iron, both were wood until the latter part of the 19th century. The large iron wheel at the later Mora stone mill remains there today (Figure 31).

On the inside surface of the pit wheel are gear teeth projecting horizontally. It is this gear that meshes with a companion gear whose teeth are vertical (or angular) that transfers the mechanical force of the turning vertical waterwheel to the turning horizontal millstone. In early mills both sets of teeth were made of heavy wooden dowels, since the potential shifting of a good mesh or fit could easily lead to breakage and dowels can be easily replaced. Where this was the case the vertical gear was known as a lantern pinion **(Figure 29m)** driving the vertical shaft. The ease of replacement of wood gear teeth, however, is offset by the relatively rapid wear that results from continued operation. Iron gear teeth were thus much preferred, although combinations were frequently used, a horizontal gear being iron, say, whose cogs drive an adjacent gear with wood cogs.

Frequently, however, as in the case of the Taos mill, the horizontal gear teeth of the vertical pit wheel **(n)** were fabricated in sections which could be bolted on the wood wheel and easily replaced if broken. The horizontal iron gear which engages these bolted sections is beveled **(Figure 28m)**.

There are two alternative mill designs from this point upward to the mill stones. One of these designs, not illustrated here, has this gear—either a lantern pinion or a beveled pinion—indirectly engaging the millstones. This gear, in this case called a "wallower", is set on a heavy vertical shaft which rests on an iron bearing on the floor of the wheel room and passes up through the ceiling to the milling floor, and then beyond this to be fixed at a companion bearing on a strong wooden joist. Here on the second floor a larger-diameter gear wheel, the "spur wheel", on the same vertical shaft, is the preliminary driver of the milling stone. Its horizontal teeth engage the teeth of the small wheel—called the "stone nut"—attached to the shaft (called the "stone spindle") which in turn is attached directly to the top stone, the runner stone **(f)**, that grinds the grain. If there are two runs of stone at the mill, the spur wheel drives, alternatively, two stone nuts on opposite sides of its circumference, attached to two sets of stone.

In our illustrations, both the lantern pinion (Figure 29) and the beveled pinion (Figure 28) are on the stone spindle **(l)**. These gears **(m)** are thus known as stone nuts. The stone spindle is supported on a bearing attached to a movable wood bridge tree **(o)**. The bridge tree, adjustable by a spiral screw **(p)**, will raise or lower the runner stone **(f)**—called "tentering"—as it rotates against the fixed, or bedder stone **(g)**, thus regulating the texture (coarse to fine) of the product. When fully extended, the bridge tree can lift the stone nut entirely from the gear engagement with the spur wheel, thus ceasing all rotation. However, when

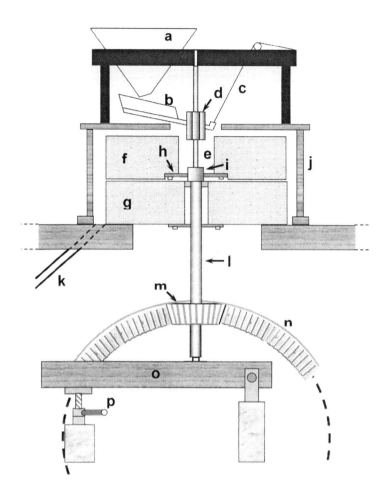

28. Schematic diagram of a typical 19th century commercial flour mill, interior view (illustration by author)

the mill is not grinding at all, the gate at the head of the flume is closed off entirely and the water diverted to a side channel away from the wheel—an action often controlled with a mechanical rod by the miller inside the mill.

The runner stone has a central hole, the eye **(e)**, that is larger than the spindle shaft, allowing grain to pass down onto the bedder surface and thus be ground. For this reason, the runner stone is carefully notched on its lower surface so as to accept a well-fitted and bolted iron plate, the rynd **(h)**, attached to a collar, the mace **(i)**, on the spindle. The two stones are protected by and enclosed in a circular wooden frame, the vat (or hoop) **(j)**

The grain is introduced into the eye by a wood shoe **(b)** which acts like a horizontal funnel, its angle of incline adjustable by a cord, the crook string **(c)**. On the adjacent shaft passing through the eye, an irregular damsel **(d)** engages the shoe in a cyclical vibration as it turns, shaking the grain into the eye. In turn, a hopper **(a)** is positioned like an inverted pyramid just above the shoe, and the miller controls the volume of grain as he fills the hopper. This entire mechanism is supported by a wood frame, the horse. The flour or meal is moved by the turning stone to its perimeter, where it travels by a chute **(k)** into a flour chest for packaging.

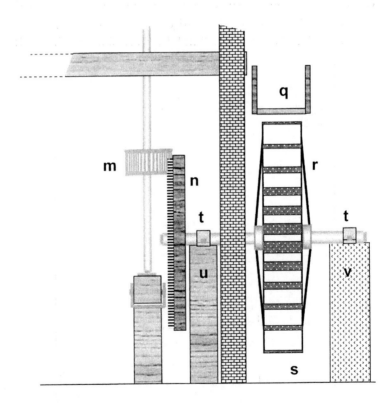

29. Schematic diagram of a typical 19th century commercial flour mill, showing millwheel (illustration by author)

Waterwheel Dimensions

The diameter of the waterwheel varied slightly among early commercial mills in New Mexico. The iron wheels at the stone mill in Mora and at the Romero mill at LaCueva are listed as twelve and fifteen feet in diameter, respectively, in the 1870 census. The other northern New Mexico mills in that year ranged from eleven and one-half feet at the Delaney mill in Mora to twelve and sixteen feet, respectively, for the Webster and the Mueller mills in Ranchos. The wheel in the Gusdorf steam mill in Ranchos, in 1880, was also sixteen feet in diameter.

Wheel widths were generally from four to six feet. The runs of stone—that is, the number of paired stones operated by a single wheel—were generally either one or two (the non-commercial Trambley mill in Las Vegas had three), and were independent of wheel size, being more a function of water power and/or stone diameter if run simultaneously. Many of the mills by the 1860s were using a much-improved millstone patented by John T. Noyes, at Noyes Mill Stone Manufacturing in Buffalo, New York.[4] The patented granite stones increased milling capacity while allowing a reduction of millstone diameter—down to three feet in some instances. Mueller and Webster, in Taos, each used these in their mills.

A decided advantage in having at least two runs of stone lay in the diversity of product. Most mills, whether grinding commercially or custom, produced not only flour for human consumption but *middlings* and other wheat by-products used for feed. A coarser and cheaper stone could be used for this without tying up a fine buhr stone.

All of the mills referenced above had overshot wheels, but other mills in the region doing only custom milling had a Leffel's turbine wheel.[5] The differences in size of the overshot wheels (if accurately reported), although minor, suggested that most had custom wooden wheel frames. Their relatively narrow widths suggest that the fall of water was sufficient most of the time. When the water source is erratic or insufficient, wider wheels with smaller diameters often provide compensation.

The Forebay, Mill Race, Mill Pit, and Water Power

The diversion of water from a river or stream for the purpose of driving a waterwheel requires a number of preparatory steps in construction and engineering. First, the diversion canal must begin at an elevation sufficiently high to provide predictable water supply. This diversion, normally in the simple form of a stone-lined ditch or *acequia*, brings water through a *headgate* into a millpond or reservoir—the *forebay*—where sufficient volume of water is stored to provide adequate water power to the millwheel even when the source is low in supply. Where the source is predictable and adequate, a sluiceway canal is alone sufficient. This latter is the case with Romero's old mill at LaCueva, in the Mora Valley, where the cement-lined sluiceway remains today.

There is sometimes a gate to this forebay to prevent flooding and allow excess water to escape via a *wasteway* back into the stream source. At its head, the forebay may have another gate, this one to control water flowing into the sluiceway which feeds the millwheel. The initial part of this sluiceway is the *headrace*. At his first mill, at Ranchos, Ceran's construction allowed the headrace an initial elevation of ten feet above the millwheel, providing substantial waterpower. The wheelpit, where the wheel turns, receives and contains the water flowing over the wheel and channels it into the *tailrace* and thence back into the stream. This wheelpit must be well-sealed on the mill side to prevent water seepage into the mill itself. It was stone lined in the Taos mill, and cemented stone blocks in the later stone mill in Mora.

Hiram Vasquez described the layout and construction of the sluiceway for the mill he and Felix St. Vrain constructed at the Francisco ranch in La Veta, Colorado. It was important to measure and control the rate of flow, and thus to know the systematic change in elevation from the point of diversion in the Cucharas River to the mill site. "The site was chosen below the brow of a hill about one hundred yards to the south" of the ranch. "Here there would be adequate fall for turning the water wheel."[6] The fall of the ditch from the diversion was decided to be six and one quarter inches per one hundred feet. With this standard, the point of diversion had to be found by proceeding upstream. Ingeniously, Hiram constructed his measuring device using a pole and surveying level:

A pole with a smooth hewn upper face and exactly sixteen feet long, was supported on one end with a leg two feet, six inches long; the leg on the other end one inch shorter. The leveling bubble was placed exactly in the center of the pole, and one arrow pointed to the shorter leg.[7]

30. Ceran's stone mill in Mora today (photograph by author)

31. Detail view of iron wheel and wheel pit, Mora (photograph by author)

Marking the points at the short end where the bubble was level provided the precise ratio of ascent. Felix cleared the line of brush, trees and rock. The Cucharas was reached a mile beyond the hill, the diversion dam was constructed, and the ditch widened and deepened until the *acequia* was done.

At Taos, too, the diversion of the Rio Grande del Rancho to provide water power for Ceran's first mill, was about one mile upstream, and the fall from the beginning of the headrace was probably about the same, but the difference in elevation between the probable diversion and the mill was less than one hundred feet. This explains the need for a forebay. Today, the stream has a healthy flow throughout much of the year, but in dry years with little spring snow melt and scarce summer rain, the stream is low and a reservoir would probably be necessary.

7
The Excavations

Ceran St. Vrain most likely constructed his Taos mill in 1849 and put it into operation in 1850. Records indicate that, while he built and operated other mills in the interim, most significantly his highly productive mill at Mora, the Taos mill continued supplying flour until 1864, when the main milling and storage rooms burned. It was re-occupied at least twice after that, being finally abandoned for good around 1903.

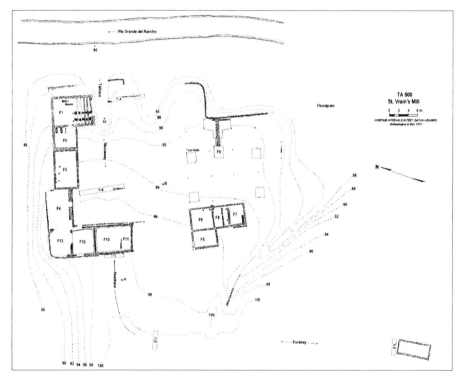

32. Map of TA 600, St. Vrain's Mill (Illustration by author)

Evidence for the chronology of use comes from excavations—architecture, stratigraphy, and artifacts—as well as from oral and documentary history.

Together, this record provides a colorful insight into a rapidly-changing 19th century economy and the role played by the U.S. military.

Subsequent to its burning in 1864, the mill was abandoned. We have no deed or bill of sale indicating that St. Vrain sold the mill, nor any evidence that he removed machinery to be used in his stone mill in Mora. Oral reports of those present during the subsequent years, however, suggest that the mill was rebuilt and in operation in the closing years of the century, but abandoned again by 1903.

During excavation, the site was visited by two elderly residents of the area who provided recollections from their childhood. Sr. Appolonio Sanchez, of Rodarte, in the nearby Peñasco Valley, recalls visiting the site as a young boy. He stated that in 1901 a small grist mill was in operation, comprising the milling room and adjacent storage structures, our Features 1-3, but that by 1903 the structures had "fallen down". He recalled that our Features 1-4 all had stone foundations with adobe walls, and that Features 10-13 constituted a single adobe building with a flat roof. He could not recall any remains of Features 5-8, suggesting that these were only in use during St. Vrain's operation. He claimed that no further use of the site was made after 1903. He and his father made regular trips to and from Taos and Rodarte, passing by the site each time. On the speculation that a sawmill operated at the site during its later history, Mr. Sanchez claimed that a sawmill did exist some distance upstream (possibly at the site of the sawmill utilized in 1852-3 by Cantonment Burgwin), but not at the mill site.

Sr. Jacob M. Bernal, of Ranchos de Taos, recalls visiting the ruins in 1911. His recollection was that the mill was shut down sometime in 1901. Unfortunately, neither man ever saw the mill in actual operation. Sr. Sanchez recalls the wooden sluiceway, but recollected the wheel as horizontal rather than vertical. As a final note, during excavations a crudely carved cornerstone was found in the fill, bearing the date "5/7/92" and the initials "JCM".

Field Methodology

The general location of St. Vrain's mill in Taos was known from military and other documents, and ongoing excavations at Cantonment Burgwin, three miles south, had long stimulated interest in locating and excavating the mill. In the summer of 1972 a small survey group actively searched for and found the site, three miles north of Burgwin and less than one hundred yards inside the northern boundary marker for Carson National Forest, on the west side of State Highway 3 (now Highway 518). A formal excavation request was submitted to the Carson, an unsystematic surface collection was made, recording the location of each item, and exposed surface features were mapped.

33. Students conducting initial surface survey, view from west (photograph by author)

Excavation began on June 11 the following year, 1973, with the author as supervisor and field school director. While a central purpose was the professional training of field archaeologists, the research goal was of equal importance, and a rigorous schedule with continual reinforcement of standards was adhered to. Two experienced field assistants, Paul Larsen and Herb Mosca, were particularly helpful in checking field work and daily records.

Two permanent benchmarks (labeled A and B on the map, Figure 32) were initially established, and a plane table and alidade were used to make a contour map of the site. All distances were chained with a metric tape, and elevations were read directly off of the stadia rod. This contour map gave the first good indication of the mill's forebay, wasteway, and sluiceway, thus guiding the excavation plan and presaging some of the interpretive conclusions.

Manual labor was exclusively employed in the excavations. Indeed, even had a backhoe been prudential, maneuvering it across the Rio Grande del Rancho would have been challenging. Excavation dirt was screened and backdirt removed from the site by wheelbarrow.

With some exceptions, excavation levels were defined in 20-centimeter units, and all artifacts were placed in collection bags labeled by level. Test trenches and squares designed to reveal in profile the patterns of silt deposition, and other features of the hydraulic system, of course did not adhere to this arbitrary level protocol. Horizontal provenience was controlled by triangulation from wall corners within architectural features, and by measuring distances from permanent markers outside such features.

The overall excavation strategy was to expose all walls first, where possible. In most cases, this was quite successful, as most of the mill was constructed using stone. Even adobe brick, where used, was generally well preserved. Apparently the stone architectural components, unlike wood flooring, roof beams, and windows, were sufficiently abundant in the region to prevent scavenging when the mill was finally abandoned.

Where walls were identified, square excavation units (often one meter square) proceeded from each corner downwards until a floor was reached- and then lower, in order to identify building and occupational sequences. This procedure was not standardized, however: opportunities for identification and recovery were dictated by the features encountered. So long as adequate horizontal and vertical control were recorded, and accurate maps were drawn, the excavators felt no obligation for blind adherence to convention.

A record of each day's excavation, by crew, was kept on Daily Field Record forms, with associated forms for maps, profiles, and other diagrams. These were supplemented by daily narrative journals with personal observations, kept by each student. Excavations generally ceased by 3-3:30 to give each person and each crew time to complete these and to reflect on the day's work. Insights from these were often key to the following day's excavation strategies.

After dinner each night, everyone assembled in the laboratory to wash, sort, identify and catalog recovered artifacts. The catalog numbers, 73 followed by numbers consecutively assigned, were written on the artifacts (or on containers in which they were placed), and on the 5 x 7 catalog cards which included provenience information and a drawing of each item.

Two weeks into the season, several architectural structures had not yet been outlined by wall exposure. Crews were diverted to identifying these structures, even though they were not excavated, and thus all of the buildings built and used during the mill's several occupation periods had their walls and corners exposed. Further work, of course, would still benefit our understanding of this important and multi-layered site.

All original field records, maps, and reports, as well as all catalogued materials, are permanently archived at the Fort Burgwin Research Center. Photographs of the excavations were developed at the Center, but negatives are archived at Southern Methodist University. Needless to say, the University encourages interested scholars to visit and study the materials.

Topography

Designated on the catalog of sites created and maintained by the Fort Burgwin Research Center as TA-600, the mill site is located three miles north of the confluence (at 7,400 ft. elevation) of the Rito de la Olla (Pot Creek) and the Rio Grande del Rancho, and less than a mile south of where the Rio Chiquito joins the latter stream (Figure 15). Together, these three streams drain the valley known as the Tres Ritos Hills. The valley is narrow but long, rising from the settlement of Talpa at its mouth, resting at 7,100 ft. in elevation, to U.S. Hill in the south, at just over 8,000 ft. The site itself stands at 7,200 ft. State Highway 518 (then Highway 3) follows the course of the Rio Grande del Rancho for most of the valley's length. When the mill was in operation, the wagon road along the valley hugged the western foothills and the river coursed along the east of the road, with one or two road crossings between the mill and Cantonment Burgwin.

The western side of the valley rises abruptly to peak elevations of 8,000 ft. in the area of the mill to 8,500 just west of the Cantonment, and does so in a horizontal distance of less than three-quarters of a mile. The mill is located on a relatively narrow terrace above the floodplain. While the eastern side of the valley is much broader to the south, as is the first terrace, at the northern location of the mill the valley is at its narrowest, with no comparable terrace for its location on the east side. Given the greater hydraulic energy, due to the river's fall, at the northern location, the mill is ideally situated to optimize water power. The eastern rise covers a much greater horizontal distance—and numerous escarpments—before reaching an elevation of 10,000 ft.

34. TA 600 prior to excavation. View from terrace east of Highway 3 (foreground). Arrow indicates original road on west side of site (photograph by author)

The valley is characterized by heavy stands of piñon pine and Rocky Mountain juniper throughout its lower terraces, increasingly dominated by ponderosa pine and some Douglas fir as the elevation approaches 7,500 ft. On the floodplain patches of giant sage and rabbitbrush are common, while red willow and cottonwood dominate the wetter zone adjacent to the permanent streams. For mill construction, therefore, wood was abundant, and local adobe deposits were more than sufficient for ample brick production.

35. The Rio Grande del Rancho in June 1973. Taken where tailrace would have re-entered (photograph by author)

Site overview

The site map (Figure 32) provides a visual overview of the several rooms—not all of them contemporary by any means—and the hydraulic features central to the initial mill operation. Information suggests that Features (rooms) 1 and 2 were the first built, and were contiguous, and that Feature 3 was added shortly thereafter. These were of the most substantial construction. The remaining features were added during subsequent operations. The forebay, headrace, and wasteway had been dug out but, aside from some stone reinforcement and channeling, had operated without further construction. The sluiceway was a wooden channel, directing the water to the over-shot wheel at the south wall of the mill house (Feature 1), and the tailrace was stone-reinforced to floodplain level, where the mill water re-entered the Rio Grande del Rancho.

In the narrative that follows, each of these features will be described in order, followed by discussion of the trenches (A-E), test units, and the several rock alignments. Description of the artifacts will follow this, concluding with an interpretive section.

Features 1-3[1]

Wall foundations

When survey and site clearing began on Features 1-3, enough of the stone walls were visible to guide in the delineation of the three rooms. Feature 1 was designated the "Mill House" from its logistical position, its greater depth relative to adjacent rooms, and the deep declivity on its south side, indicating the probable wheel pit location (Figure 36).

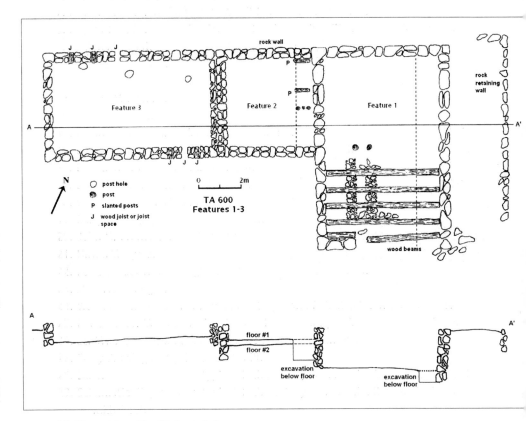

36. Plan and profile, Features 1-3

Well-dressed and layered rock defined both the northeast and northwest corners, with more intermittent rock along both the northern and eastern wall foundations. The most substantial wall remains consisted of layered cut stone ranging from a meter to a meter and a half in height. Of the south wall, very little remained, as it bounded the almost vertical drop where the tailrace began.

In Feature 2, the north and west walls were more fragmentary than those of the mill house, although similarly dressed. Uniform adobe brick remnants were found atop the stone foundation of the entire west wall, indicating that this wall, at least, was made of adobe brick. Chunks of fallen adobe scattered in the fill of Features 1, 2, and 3 suggest the same for all of the walls. The wall separating Features 1 and 2 was fragmentary and intermittent, as was the south wall of Feature 2. There was evidence that much of it had collapsed due to the steepness of the adjacent slope from west to east, falling approximately 2m. over a 2m. horizontal distance.

Feature 2 shares a common north wall with Feature 3, although it was more fragmentary. To its common boundary wall with Feature 3, a thin cobble wall had apparently been added on the west side.

Interpretation of the construction of these three features is aided in part by analysis of the type and quality of stone construction. In Feature 1, predominantly large stones had been selected, and these were dressed to present a relatively smooth face (although no apparent intentional shaping of the top or bottom surfaces). In Feature 2, all surfaces of the rock were more smoothly prepared, and stones of various sizes had been positioned so as to produce a more uniformly compact wall. The irregular south and west wall surfaces of Feature 3 indicate a more random and less careful selection of building material, including smaller stone. These were also less carefully dressed to fit one another. At the time of initial construction, this feature may well have been an enclosed courtyard or ramada, with the sturdier north wall perhaps providing more solid protection at the edge of the adjacent arroyo (Figure 37). The cobble wall on the east of Feature 3 was thicker at its base, suggesting reinforcement to hold an eventual roof. There was no evidence of small-stone chinking or of mortar in any of the wall construction.

37. View north into arroyo from Feature 3 prior to excavation (photograph by author)

Upper Walls

The fill of these three rooms gives no indication of fallen stone from wall collapse. This most likely indicates that the second (post-1865) occupation—and probably the original as well—had walls of wood and/or adobe built on the stone foundations.

Inasmuch as fire destroyed the mill's superstructure in 1864, an original wall of adobe brick would have partially collapsed as the roof burned and fell in, leaving sizable burned and fire hardened adobe debris, which was not found. The adobe bricks on the west wall foundation of Feature 3, and the unburned chunks of adobe fill in all rooms, suggests that the post-fire re-use of the partially-collapsed mill included adobe wall construction.

Complicating these interpretations is the knowledge, supplied by Mr. Sanchez, that when the site was finally abandoned for good, locals scavenged all of the usable materials, including vigas and adobe bricks.

Room Fill

It is obvious that evidence of upper wall construction from the room fill of Features 1-3 represent the final phase of construction and abandonment.

Mr. Sanchez recalled that in 1901 Features 1 and 2 were of equal height and of adobe construction typical for this area. He did not recall Feature 3.

The fill profile gives some indication of the events that occurred during and after the final occupation. Since Feature 1 had a lower floor below ground level and was thus deeper than the adjacent Feature 2, there was considerable blown dust, deposited silt and discarded post-occupation debris in this room. The fill was primarily loam or sandy top soil mixed with manmade trash and collapsed stone from the wall foundations. Rusted tin cans piled in the northeast and northwest corners possibly reflect more recent use by transients, as do the charcoal fragments common in the surface fill. No adobe or consolidated, packed earth was found in the fill. Occasional thin layers of wheat were found below the fill at floor level where stone and wood fragments were located, most likely adjacent to the grist stones.

Feature 2 fill stratigraphy revealed, on the east side and southwest corner, the probable existence of two occupation layers. Alternative layers of soft sandy loam, packed earth with adobe chunks, and an ash-sawdust layer are shown in the profile. Floor I (the upper floor layer related to the later occupation) is relatively well marked by a 5-10 cm thick layer of sawdust, chaff, and wood scrap revealed in each corner of the room as well as in the north-south trench which was excavated to test the depth of occupation. Modern drawn nails were common above this layer. Floor II (the probable St. Vrain mill occupation) is marked by a stratum of ash and charcoal which appears 10-23 cm thick near the north wall, thinning out as one approaches the south side of the room, but marked there by an adobe-like floor of hard-packed clay. Older square nails were mixed in the ash of this burned layer.

The northeast corner of Feature 2 appears to have been a storage pit excavated in the floor, with sloping juniper poles supporting the adjacent floor above. The plan drawing shows the post holes demarcating the northern wall of this pit. Chunks of fallen adobe were found along the north and west walls of the most recent occupation. Rodent and anthill disturbance across much of the surface had destroyed some of the original context.

Feature 3 revealed only a single occupational layer with wood scrap debris above it. Mixed fill of adobe, rocks, sawed wood planks, small wood scraps and sawdust covered the excavated portions of this room beneath the later surface dirt. Fragments of floor joists were found in the northwest and southeast corners.

The nature of the fill suggests that this feature may have been part of a sawmill operation, referenced in several deed and property transfer documents without giving adequate location. If this were the case, Feature 3 was not contemporaneous with the original mill operation, an interpretation further supported by the reinforced wall adjacent to Feature 2.

Doorways and Windows

Only circumstantial evidence indicates possible locations for these room features. In Feature 1 there are two possible door openings: on the west wall south of but next to the south wall of Feature 2, and between these two features towards the south end of the wall separating them.

The former is indicated only by an apparent break in the stone foundation, although fragmentary evidence prevented determination of whether the break was intentional or due to collapse and shifting. The latter location also has a break in the wall foundation with an adjacent adobe surface which could mark a step or a vestibule. A metal hinge and door plate were found in the room fill of Feature 1 directly below this spot. The test trench dug parallel to the east wall in Feature 2 also revealed, just north of the adobe "step", three post holes suggesting a partition providing a vestibule at the entryway. North of this were two slanted posts, with their tops at the west wall of the trench, possibly representing a storage bin.

Window glass distribution is the only good evidence for window location. In the southwest corner of Feature 1 a concentration of window glass was found in the fill, indicating a possible window in one of the two walls. Likewise, in Feature 2, window glass concentrations were found in the southwest and northeast corners. In the latter location glass was abundant, while in the former only ten pieces were found, together with some small wood fragments of a size appropriate for framing. Of course, the most likely scavenging after site abandonment would be for windows, so the lack of glass debris is no indication of the absence of windows.

Floors and Roofs

In Feature 1 the remnants of five large floor joists laid parallel to the waterwheel were found in the southern half of the room. These became more fragmentary towards the north, so it seems likely that they ran originally across the entire floor. Remains of floor boards in the southeast corner suggests that plank flooring covered the joists. Below the joists beginning at the south wall lay two parallel rows of flat stones on either side of the supposed location of the main drive shaft, probably to support the heavy machinery on the floor above.

In Feature 2, both occupation levels had packed-earth floors, at places as firm and fine textured as puddled adobe, but lacking the latter's color and composition.

Feature 3 apparently had a traditional joist-and-plank floor. Here, floor joists ran north-south across the narrow room width for its extensive length. These joists were firmly anchored by the stone walls into which they were carefully fitted, and rested on tamped earth beneath. Earth apparently filled the spaces between, finished with planking laid directly on the earth and nailed to the joists. In places, the earth was hard-packed and could have served as the final floor without planking. This earth had become fire-reddened, hardened with clay along the north wall.

Also along the north wall were three post holes, approximately 6-8 inches in diameter, spaced evenly from west to east but diverging from the wall in that direction (the first directly against the wall). Their function is not known.

According to witnesses around 1900 the three features were "adobe and stone rooms", of traditional construction. Sr. Sanchez recalled that the roofs were flat with no pitch, and thus probably adobe laid on latillas and vigas. These, of course, would have been scavenged.

Room Functions

It is interesting to note that no certain evidence for fireplaces was found during excavations. Among any other features, both adobe and stone fireplaces would have been well-preserved had they ever been present. This is testified by the well-preserved hearths at nearby Cantonment Burgwin, which was occupied by the military from 1852 through early 1860.[2] This negative evidence would support the interpreted use of these rooms for commercial or business purposes rather than residential.

There is little doubt that Feature 1 was the milling room. The adjacent sluiceway and tailrace provide ample evidence for the position of a vertical wheel outside the south wall. A keyed iron shaft, 161 cm in length and 15 cm in diameter, was found near the bottom of the tailrace adjacent to the south wall. A gear and fragments of a leather belt used for belt-drive gears, together with a small collection of wheat seed, were found at floor level in Feature 1, approximately one meter from the excavation surface. At the southwest location where floor planks were discovered was a small amount of grease. This evidence, and additional items to be discussed in the artifact section, points to the presumed milling function for Feature 1. Support posts and upper floor joists were missing from the fill, and were likely scavenged upon abandonment.

Feature 2 was, at least in its early phase, likely to have been used for grain storage. Evidence includes fragments of burlap sacking, wheat chaff, and well-preserved grain heads. Randomly scattered piles of axe-cut wood chips, kindling-size wood, and assorted metal and china fragments were also found here.

Interpreting Feature 3 is more problematical. Remains of cut lumber, possibly 2 x 4 pieces, were found stacked in the northeast corner, suggesting a possible sawmill, workshop, or storage room. The three vertical post holes along the north wall, as previously noted, are somewhat anachronistic.

Features 5-8[3]

This L-shaped complex is separated from the south wall of Feature 10 by a distance of 12 meters. Both exterior and interior walls had stone foundations (Figure 38). In general, the fill throughout was composed of three layers. From surface to approximately 10-15 cm in depth was a layer of fine, sandy and largely windblown soil. Below this was a hard-packed grayish-brown soil measuring 15-30 cm in depth. Extending from this point to the floor was a layer of fine, dark-brown peaty loam about 15-25 cm thick. Scattered throughout were fragments of wood, charcoal, adobe chunks, and burned earth. Also present were thick fragments of *tierra blanca*[4] wall plaster, some of it painted and some with attached wallpaper.

Wall Foundations

The architecture basically consisted of a stone foundation, two stones thick, for each of the four rooms. Large cornerstones were found at several wall corners, and the upper surface of the wall foundations had a relatively even layer of gray mortar, indicating that stone or adobe walls were present throughout. Absence of post holes anywhere in the foundation makes it unlikely that log or wooden walls were constructed.

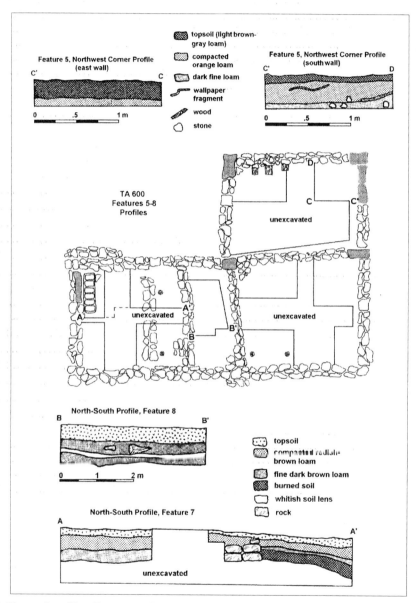

38. Plan and profiles, Features 5-8

The rooms were not laid out in any regular manner and few corners were 90 degrees. The most erratic room was Feature 8, with its east and north walls meeting at an angle of 80 degrees, and its north and west walls at 100 degrees.

39. Feature 6 walls before excavation. Note 19th century road in background (photograph by author)

The walls and room fill indicate that three periods of construction characterized the complex, although all three occurred during a relatively brief period of time. Features 7 and 8 were probably constructed together originally, with a wall located midway between them. This fragmented wall, when excavated, did not reach the east or west walls, indicating that it had been demolished and a floor built over the foundation. Two postholes were located on the east and west perimeters of this wall against its north side. Their functions are unknown. A fragment of a west wall of stone lay just west of the later wall and was probably part of the original construction as well. The north wall of Feature 8 was built erratically.

A second period involved the demolition of the wall dividing the original structure and the construction of the last Feature 8 south wall and the addition of Feature 6. The resulting Feature 8 was little more than a meter wide in its north-south dimension, useful only as a vestibule or storage closet. This narrower room also did not apparently last long, for its abutment with the east and west walls lacked some stones when excavated.

The final phase saw the construction of Feature 5, whose walls abut Feature 6 where the latter features' large cornerstones provide obvious points of contact. These construction periods are further indicated by non-contiguous floors.

Room Fill and Floors

The general nature of fill throughout the shallow rooms consisted of gray, fine, sandy topsoil, much of it windblown sand, in the first 15 cm, followed by compacted gray-brown earth, 15-30 cm, and below this fine, dark-brown peaty loam down to floor level at 15-25 cm. Scattered through this, of course, was human made debris. Most identifiable wood pieces were not thick enough for roof timbers, and joist fragments underlay most of the smaller pieces.

Feature 5 had a joist-and-plank floor, with at least some of the joists anchored within the foundation stone. Plank fragments were scattered in the fill. Round nails of various sizes exceeded square nails 2-to-1. In addition, a tight cluster of 177 4d round nails was found in the fill. A small concentration of window glass was found in the northwest corner.

Feature 6 had indications of two tamped-earth floors, below room fill, in the southwest corner. Between these was evidence of planking, and in the southeast corner as well. Window glass was found both outside and inside the north wall from one to two meters from the northeast corner. Two post holes were located just inside the east wall, about 50 cm from and parallel to the east wall along its southern half. Their function is unknown.

Feature 7 had the most extensive floor evidence, extending over 2/3 of the room to the south wall, and consisted of compacted reddish-brown loam. However, a cluster of wooden planks in the southwest corner of the room indicates a wooden overlay. At 20 cm, this plank floor overlays the original stone wall foundation which separated Features 7 and 8, further testifying to the building sequence discussed earlier. The northern 1/3 was excavated to sterile at 60 cm with no indication of a floor.

Window glass indicated possible windows on the west wall, 2 meters from the southwest corner, and on the east wall, 2 meters from the southeast corner.

A north-south profile in Feature 8 revealed a whitish-colored soil lens 50-65 cm from surface, along the middle of fine dark-brown loam (55 cm thick) overlaid by topsoil. No floor was in evidence, nor any remains of window glass.

Doorways

A probable doorway was located at the northwest corner of the north wall in Feature 5, where two large dressed stones were placed in the foundation and could have served as a threshold. Midway along the common wall with Feature 7, the foundation stones show a slight depression and a flattened wear pattern which could also reflect a doorway. It is certainly likely that access between the rooms would have been provided when Feature 5 was added. In Feature 6 itself, there is no evidence of exterior doors, nor of a doorway in the south wall. Near the southwest corner of the south wall of Feature 7, a likely exterior door is indicated by a large dressed stone in the foundation wall and six aligned adobe bricks just inside the room, resting on the adobe floor. Feature 8 had no indications of any doorways.

Room Functions

Much of the artifact recovery in all of these rooms points to a domestic use. By far the majority of wallpaper fragments, some directly on wall plaster fragments, were found in these features. Almost all toy fragments and a good many of the recovered buttons, as well as most beads and other jewelry items, came from these rooms, as did a large portion of china pieces. Despite the absence of indications of any fireplaces, the strong suggestion is that these rooms were a domestic household.

Both Sr. Sanchez and Sr. Bernal could not recall these features during their boyhood visits to the area in 1901. The dates of these occupations will be discussed after artifact evidence has been presented. At this point it is fascinating to note that one of the final occupations took place at the close of the 19th century: an Indian head penny bearing the date 1881 was discovered in Feature 5 at the 0-20 cm level.

It ought to be additionally noted that the absence of an adobe or stone fireplace is not negative evidence of household occupation. Cast iron heating and cooking stoves were in common use in the Taos area beginning in the 1850s.

Features 4, 10-13[5]

Time constraints prevented extensive excavation of these features. The excavation focused on careful delineation of all walls and wall areas (Figure 40). Probing for floors was not done, but fill was excavated generally to depths of 15-30 cm. Two of the features were likely not roofed rooms, and were more than likely walled courtyards or work areas. A heavy collection of charcoal, with burned stone, in the northeast portion of Feature 13, suggests a forge or similar source of fire, rather than a hearth. Likewise, in the center of Feature 4 was a large (1 x ½ meter) patch of burned earth, and a deposit of ash and charcoal was found near the south wall. Room fill included horseshoes, nails, and a horse's hoof. This feature, too, could have housed a blacksmith operation.

Wall Foundations

Feature 4 is bounded on the north by a stone retaining wall, two stones wide, which continues to border Feature 13 as well. The site map indicates the steep elevation decline along the north side of these features, defining the side of an arroyo—almost a ten-foot drop in the horizontal distance of 7 m. (see Figure 37). This retaining wall, which averages 41 cm in width, appears to abruptly curve south at the northwest corner of Feature 13 to provide part of the west wall, although the stones here had been seriously disturbed and many were missing. The site map is speculative at this corner.

At the northeast corner is a 150 cm gap separating the retaining wall from the west wall of Feature 3. A short row of adobe bricks represents what was apparently an adobe wall on the west side, forming the dividing wall between Features 4 and 13. On the south side of Feature 4 is a stone wall just over 8 m. in length, averaging 83 cm in thickness, with the southernmost stone row continuing west to an apparent outside corner with Feature 12.

Large amounts of plaster and *tierra blanca* were found along the boundary between Features 4 and 13, indicating that an adobe wall did indeed define this boundary. Decayed wood in substantial amounts characterized the fill of Feature 4, including tree bark, indicating the use of vigas for the roof.

A line of adobe clumps, many in the form of crude or melted bricks, defines the wall separating Features 12 and 13. A similar row running north-

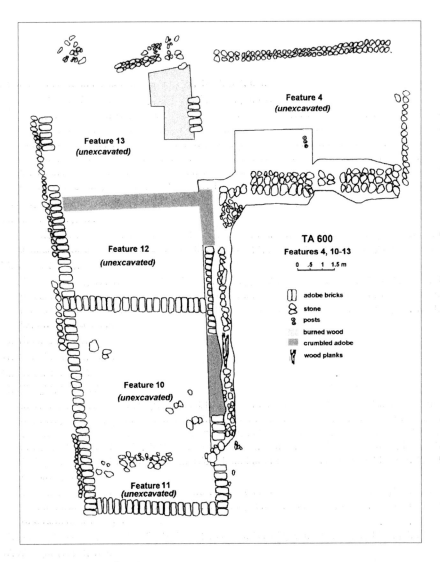

40. Plan of Features 4, 10-13

south a short distance forms part of the east wall, but within one meter is met with well-formed adobe bricks which form most of the east wall of Feature 12 and continue uninterrupted as the first half-meter of Feature 10. Here it is interrupted again by crumbled adobe for 3-1/2 meters before adobe bricks once more continue the east wall to its corner. A remnant of retaining wall lay against the outside of this wall from Feature 12 through Feature 10 and shortly beyond. This stone wall has occasional remnants of wood reinforcement.

The west wall of these features is a discontinuous row of adobe bricks with remnants of a similar stone retaining wall against the outside. The pattern of wall abutments suggests that Features 10 and 12 were built as a single partitioned structure, and possibly Features 4 and 13 were constructed then as well. Feature 11 was cleared enough to determine that it was a functional construction, but time did not permit more than cursory excavation.

Doorways and Windows

There were few doorways in evidence within the foundations. One was located in the east wall of Feature 10, indicated by a gap in the adobe foundation about 1-1/2 meters from the south corner. The center of the south wall of Feature 4 had a foundation gap of 1-1/2 meters, indicating the presence of a doorway. Doors between the rooms would certainly have been likely, but foundations were generally too poor to indicate this.

Room Functions

It is problematic whether Features 4 and 13 were actually rooms, although the south wall of Feature 4 was a substantial one and possible viga remains indicates a roof. The absence of north walls for Features 4 and 13, even though retention wall stones were still in place, is a mystery. Insufficient stones were found in the adjacent arroyo to indicate wall debris. A dividing wall between these two features might suggest a separation of function, and the plaster certainly indicates that one of these two rooms was enclosed. As noted, either of these features could have housed a blacksmith shop and would have been covered but open along the north side.

Sr. Sanchez and Sr. Bernal recall this adobe walled and single-roofed four-room structure being present in 1901 and report the entire site abandoned in 1903. When these features were constructed is not known, but they could not have been present during St. Vrain's mill operation, nor during any subsequent mill use featuring an overshot wheel, as Feature 10 sits astride the headrace where the waters would have entered the sluiceway, undoubtedly marked by a wooden flume.

Trenches A-E and Features 9, 14

The trenches were designed to help establish and confirm mill hydrology. Other than the surface contours, there was little superficial evidence for the normal components of the hydrologic run-up to the mill wheel operation: the forebay, headrace, and sluiceway were provisionally located based on these contours and the location and orientation of Features 1-3. Furthermore, even the contours were problematic in locating the forebay, as no basin with retaining walls was found. Indeed, the only retaining walls found were on the north where a deep arroyo bounded the site, and along the floodplain on the east boundary. Not all mills had forebays, of course. The Romero mill at La Cueva is a good case in point. The same was true of St. Vrain's stone mill at Mora (seen in Figure 19). At the current site, however, a forebay was in all likelihood a requirement, as the Rio Grande del Rancho frequently has a much reduced water supply in late summer—specifically at harvest time.

Trench A

Near the northeast perimeter of the site, directly across the tailrace from Feature 1, Trench A was placed perpendicular to the water flow on the promontory which bounds the tailrace's south side. The depth of trash in this trench indicates that this peninsula is largely human-made, and the mixture of water-borne deposits suggests that much of the fill came from the adjacent floodplain, probably indicated by the westward cut into the terrace just south of this peninsula.

The profile (Figure 43) shows the various layers of gravel—graded fine to coarse—sand, silt, and silty-loam. Evidence of stone retaining walls was found in the northern end of the west profile and through much of the eastern profile, together with remains of horizontal and upright logs and wood planking. This, combined with the exposed stone retaining wall at the eastern perimeter of this peninsula, suggests parallel wood-stone-earthworks designed to forestall erosion. A similar stone retaining wall east of Feature 1 served the same purpose. Trenching was also done along the south wall of the tailrace. Here, large stones and heavy wooden beam remains testify to an outboard pier in support of the bearing for the water wheel drive shaft. Throughout the fill of Trench A, and this adjacent perpendicular trench, is human trash: glass, nails, bone, charcoal, and broken china.

41. Trench A (extension). Excavators are in the wheel pit. Cross-wall in background separates Features 1 and 2 (photograph by author)

Trench B

This trench was located adjacent to the west wall of Feature 3 and ran in a north-south direction, cutting across a depression in the ground contour where the sluice was located. The profile of this trench (Figure 44) clearly shows the layers of water-deposited materials, including the fine silt and clay which settled at the bottom of the depression. Consolidated trash on either side of the depression may indicate artificial levees to prevent runoff from the dripping flume above it from entering the nearby structures.

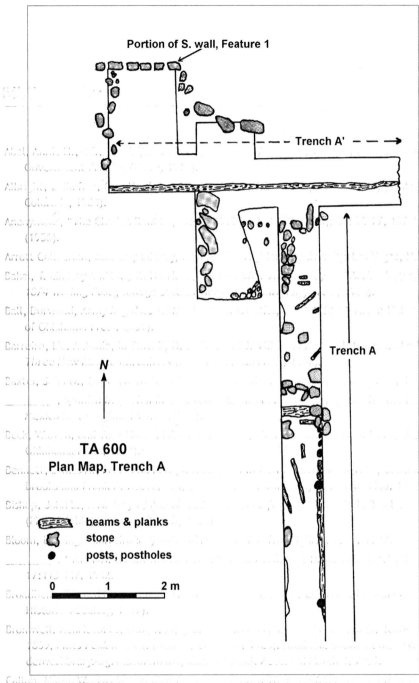

Portion of S. wall, Feature 1

Trench A'

Trench A

N

TA 600
Plan Map, Trench A

beams & planks
stone
posts, postholes

0   1   2 m

42. Plan of Trench A and extension

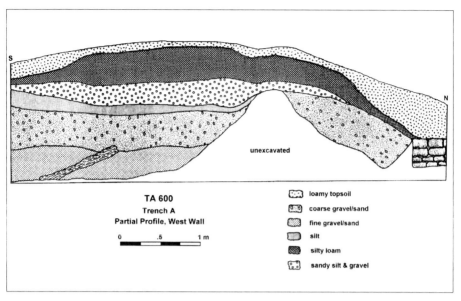

43. Profile, west wall of Trench A

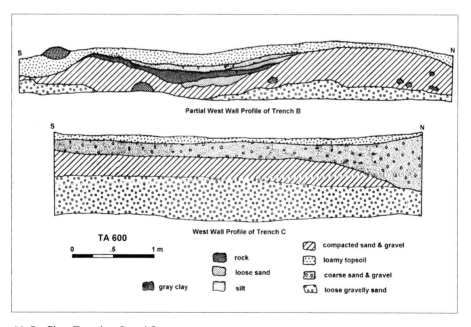

44. Profiles, Trenches B and C

A fragmentary stone wall in the southern part of the trench began 7 m. from the north end and continued for a distance of 2.6 m. It measured 50 cm in width. This was likely part of the support structure for the wooden flume.

Trench C

This trench was dug adjacent to the west wall of Feature 10, for a distance of 4.5 m., and was just over half a meter in width. Its depth was one meter (Figure 44). The profile was drawn from the exposure in the trench's west wall. Below the topsoil layer, a water-deposited layer of loose gravel and sand runs across the trench, dipping slightly in the center. Below this is a more compact layer of the same, separated by a thin layer of water-worn pebbles. The compact layer is banded with finer deposits.

At the northern end of the trench is a large concentration of large stones and pebbles. These may have been part of a flume support, or may have lined the depression to help prevent erosion.

Bordering the eastern trench wall in a north-south line is a row of adobe brick at a depth of 9 cm. This is the wall foundation for Feature 10, and indicates that it was constructed after the sluiceway and flume had been abandoned and water no longer flowed in it.

Trench D

This trench is located on the western perimeter of the site and at the high point of the site terrace, just south of the probable 90-degree turn of the water course at the beginning of the presumed headrace. Its east-west axis is 4 meters in length. Its width was 83 cm and the depth was 79 cm. (Fig 45)

Here there was an obvious depression in the center, with a thick layer of gravel banded with different sized particles. Below this is a deposit of fine silt, substantially thicker on the east side. Below this is dull-red to yellow-white clay. The thicker silt on the east side can be explained by the abrupt change in flow direction immediately north of this, in which finer materials would have been deposited on the inner turn where the water was slower, and heavier gravels deposited on the outer turn with faster-flowing water.

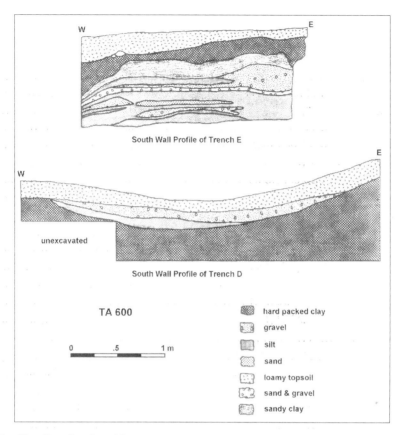

W

E

South Wall Profile of Trench E

E

W

unexcavated

South Wall Profile of Trench D

TA 600

	hard packed clay
	gravel
	silt
	sand
	loamy topsoil
	sand & gravel
	sandy clay

0   .5   1 m

45. Profiles, Trenches D and E

Several pieces of glass were found throughout the trench, along with a few animal bones and part of a clay pipe. The original surface, excavated as part of the water course, would have been the clay. There was no evidence of a retain wall, despite the trench extending through both sides of the water course.

Trench E

This trench was located at the opposite end of the presumptive forebay from Trench D. Its position was dictated by the stone foundation of Feature 14 to the immediate south. The trench was just over 2 meters long and 1 meter deep.

At the bottom of this trench, above sterile soil, was a laminated layer of silt. Interfingering in this layer are lenses of sand and small gravel. This banding had a depth of 50 to 60 cm, above which was a layer sandy clay and, above this, a layer of hard-packed clay. The top layer, just under the topsoil, was a gravel-clay mixture.

The depth of the silt deposit indicates a long period of standing water, typical of a holding pond. Below-surface testing of the perimeter of this presumed forebay was not done, and the presence of any levee or retaining walls was not ascertained. On the surface, however, no such alteration of the terrace was in evidence. The only exception was a raised berm three feet above the surface and perpendicular to the forebay on its eastern perimeter. Adjacent to and east of this begins a deep defile which probably served as a wasteway, disgorging excess forebay water into the floodplain below (Figure 32) This berm was almost certainly associated with a gate that diverted water from entering the headrace.

Feature 9

This feature was part of a test grid laid out in the flat area of the terrace between Features 5-8 on the west and the retaining wall at the floodplain on the east. This grid consisted of five-meter-squares laid out over the area, within which five 2 x 2 m. test pits were designated. Feature 9 is the only one of these excavated, and this excavation was extended to the east and expanded.

The stone retaining wall which follows the escarpment contouring the floodplain is illustrated on the site map. It ran in an uninterrupted line about 14 meters in overall length and 25 to 30 cm wide. An extension to the east of the Feature 9 test pit recovered a row of adobe bricks, 20 cm below surface, adjacent to this regaining wall and measuring four meters in length. At the same level, near the center of the adobes, lay an alignment of stones perpendicular to and abutting the stone wall. Half a meter wide, this row of stones proceeds west for about six meters, stopping at the eastern wall of the original Feature 9 test pit. It is unknown what function this wall might have served. Associated artifacts did not permit assigning a construction period to this feature.

Feature 14

Most of the stone walls of this structure were very fragmentary, except for the north. Here, 14 large stones defined the north wall, together with a 48 cm wood plank below the surface. The stones begin just 5 cm below ground level and extend downward 35 cm. This suggests a connection between this room and the forebay, but this is unlikely. If it had served to contain a headgate, there would have been evidence of a water diversion from the stream, and there was none. The perimeter was excavated but not the fill, and no identifiable cultural debris was recovered.

8
The Artifacts

More than 1600 catalogued artifacts were recovered from the excavations, in addition to prodigious amounts of wood fragments, window glass, and nails. An additional quantity of bottle glass and china fragments too small to catalog was recorded but not saved. Perishable items included wallpaper, leather, burlap, and clothing fabric. While a majority of these items were not useful in distinguishing early from late periods of occupation, a few were quite decisive and aided measurably in our interpretations. All artifacts are archived at the Fort Burgwin Research Center and are available for further study.

Part of the summer of 2007 was devoted to analyzing and photographing the artifacts and conducting comparative studies. Prior studies of the recovered materials from Cantonment Burgwin excavations helped to establish the availability and popularity of eastern U.S. items brought over the Santa Fe Trail during the 1850s. In the sections that follow, only significant finds are illustrated or described. Rather than discussing these strictly by the material of which they are made, as is frequently the custom, they will be discussed in functional units.

Mechanical

This category consists of all artifacts which could be reasonably ascribed as relating to machinery or the support structures for such machinery. A few, also included, consist of door latches or hinges. The majority of artifacts in this category, but not all, are made of iron. A total of forty-five items were catalogued.

Gears and Gear Fragments (Figure 46)

Six gears or fragments, all of cast iron, were found during excavations. Five of these came from bevel gears, such as those used to transfer from horizontal to vertical shaft operation, such as a wallower (see Figure 28m). Three of the five were found in Feature 1, as might be expected, one came from feature 4, and one was in the fill of Feature 9. The complete example pictured (Figure 46d) has an outer diameter of 19 cm, a shaft hole 4.2 cm in diameter, and a key slot 1 cm wide and 0.5 cm deep. The thickness of the gear at the shaft hole is 6 cm.

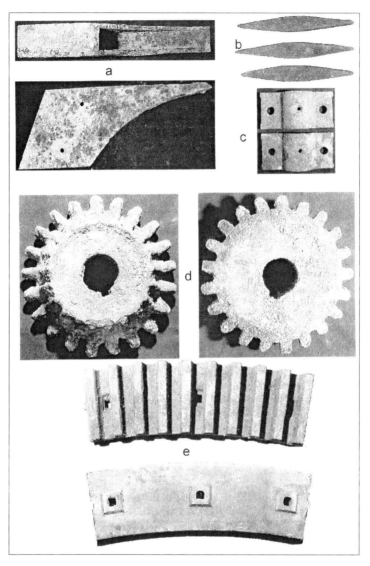

46. Mechanical iron artifacts

A gear segment (Figure 46e) from what was likely the pit wheel was recovered from Feature 6, level 2 (20-30 cm from surface). These gear segments, however, have teeth on the side rather than on the edge (as in a spur gear).

The estimated circumference is 5.4 meters, with an inner diameter of 3.12 meters. This would be appropriate for either the water wheel itself or, more likely, the pit wheel, as illustrated in Figure 28n. To make the circumference, 18 segments would have been used. This one weighs approximately 80 pounds, giving the total wheel weight—*minus the material* for the wheel itself—nearly 1500 pounds.

Drive Shaft

A cast iron shaft 1.61 meters in length and 15 cm in diameter was found in Feature 1. A keyway 3.5 cm wide and 0.8 cm in depth runs almost the entire length.

Iron Wedges

Three of these double-wedges (Figure 46b) were found, two in Feature 1 and one in Feature 4. Wedges were used in early commercial mills to adjust the bridge tree, and thus the gap between the runner stone and the bedder stone, but these were not normally double wedges as seen here. More likely, these were machine keys used to fix a pinion gear (or other gear) to a drive shaft. The wedges are 21 cm in length, 0.9 cm deep, and 3.4 cm wide. They fit nicely into the keyway of the shaft described above.

Iron Mounts

Four iron braces were found in the excavations, three from Feature 1. Two of these are half-circle shaft mounts (Figure 46c), forerunners of the more precise pillow-block, to secure a turning shaft, either horizontal or vertical, on both of its ends to a support frame. The inside diameter of the mount is 4.5 cm. A wooden shaft block mount was also found in Feature 1, capable of housing a shaft 4 cm in diameter.

An iron brace for a wooden joist or beam (Figure 46a) was found in Trench B, and was possibly used to secure the frame flume support. Its opening would have held a 3 x 10 cm wooden beam.

Drive Belts

A total of eleven leather drive belt fragments were recovered from

Features 1-4. All have from 2 to 5 holes, frequently in rows but not evenly spaced, apparently for fasteners to connect with other belt segments. Holes range most commonly 4-7 mm in diameter. Belt widths are mostly between 84 and 96 mm.

47. Leather drive belt fragments

Door Hardware

Door hardware included two hinges, one in Feature 1 and the other in Feature 9, two door latches, one in Feature 4 and the other in Feature 6, and a sill or lintel plate, 9.5 x 15.5 cm, with a keyed circular opening 4.2 cm in diameter. Fragments of wood adhered to one side. This is reminiscent of the use of pintle hinges in the early 19th Century in Taos when iron was scarce, the pintle extensions of the door stile inserting into holes in both lintel and sill. Similar plates were used well into the 20th Century to hinge heavy swinging doors.

Miscellaneous Iron

Two iron cranks were found, one with wooden handle attached, in Feature 1, and the other, with iron shaft and handle, in Feature 4. A large iron ring, 29 cm in outside diameter and 24 cm inside, was found in Feature 1. It was slightly tapered, and was 2.5 cm thick. An apparent meter cover, 7.5 cm in diameter and bearing the notation "C & D 2", was found in Feature 2.

In addition to these items, bolts (13), spikes (19), screws (8), nuts, washers, chain fragments, heavy staples, and other hardware items were found throughout the excavations. The bolts range from 2.5 to 11.3 cm in length, averaging 2 cm in diameter. The spikes range from 7.4 to 20.8 cm in length, but the majority (15) are from 10.5 to 13 cm, and all of them range from 1 to 2.5 cm in diameter.

Nails

Round (wire or machine-made) and square (or cut) nails were equally abundant in the excavations, indicating substantially different periods of use and occupation of the site. The total for both is 900 whole nails, with 491 wire nails and 409 cut nails, not including a small number of hand-forged horse-shoe nails. In addition, numerous nail fragments were recovered. The whole nails are tabulated in Tables 4 and 5 by the English penny size (abbreviated *d*) in common use then and now.

Feature	2d	3d	4d	5d	6d	7d	8d	9d	10d	12d	16d	20d	Total	%
1	-	-	7	1	4	2	10	2	4	-	1	1	32	7.8
2	1	11	10	5	3	1	7	2	4	3	-	1	48	11.7
3	-	-	1	1	6	2	6	1	-	-	-	-	17	4.2
4	3	1	3	1	3	11	18	3	9	23	-	-	75	18.3
5	-	-	-	-	3	1	1	-	-	4	2	-	11	2.7
6	-	-	8	1	-	-	11	-	4	2	3	-	29	7.1
7	-	1	4	-	4	1	15	-	5	1	-	-	31	7.8
8	-	-	-	-	-	-	3	-	2	3	1	-	9	2.2
9	1	7	21	1	25	4	42	2	19	3	-	-	125	30.6
10	-	-	1	-	1	-	-	-	-	-	-	-	2	0.5
11	-	-	-	-	1	2	6	3	1	-	-	1	14	3.4
12	-	-	-	-	-	-	-	-	-	-	-	-	0	0.0
Tr A	-	-	-	-	2	2	4	1	2	-	1	-	12	2.9
Tr B	-	-	1	-	-	-	-	1	1	-	-	-	3	0.7
Tr C	-	-	-	-	1	-	-	-	-	-	-	-	1	0.2
Totals	*5*	*20*	*56*	*10*	*53*	*26*	*123*	*15*	*51*	*39*	*8*	*3*	*409*	*100.0*
%	1.2	4.9	13.7	2.4	13.0	6.4	30.1	3.7	12.5	9.5	2.0	0.7		

Table 4. Cut nail distribution by size and feature.

Feature	2d	3d	4d	5d	6d	7d	8d	9d	10d	12d	16d	20d	Total	%
1	-	5	13	2	1	1	15	1	12	16	8	4	78	15.9
2	-	1	12	-	3	-	10	-	7	4	1	3	41	8.4
3	-	1	31	2	1	-	1	1	2	2	-	-	41	8.4
4	-	-	15	-	1	-	2	-	4	11	2	-	25	5.1
5	1	2	177	3	1	2	5	-	5	4	-	-	200	40.7
6	-	2	9	1	-	-	6	-	3	3	-	1	25	5.1
7	-	1	8	-	1	-	4	-	8	6	3	1	32	6.5
8	-	-	1	-	-	1	1	-	4	-	2	-	9	1.8
9	-	3	3	3	-	-	-	-	2	1	1	2	15	3.1
10	-	1	1	-	-	-	-	-	-	-	-	-	2	0.4
11	-	1	3	-	-	-	-	1	-	2	1	-	8	1.6
12	-	-	-	-	-	-	2	-	1	-	1	-	4	0.8
Tr A	-	2	-	2	-	-	1	-	1	2	-	2	10	2.0
Tr B	-	-	-	-	-	-	-	-	-	-	-	1	1	0.2
Tr C	-	-	-	-	-	-	-	-	-	-	-	-	0	0.0
Totals	1	19	273	12	8	4	47	3	49	41	19	14	491	100.0
%	0.2	3.9	55.6	2.6	1.6	0.8	9.6	0.6	10.0	8.4	3.9	2.9		

Table 5. Wire nail distribution by size and feature.

Machine-cut square nails, appearing in the mid-18th Century in the American colonies, became widely available on the frontier in the early 19th Century and replaced the hand-forged varieties in demand from blacksmiths. Wire nails did not become commercially available on the western frontier until the early 1900s, thus providing a good benchmark for dating the occupational periods.

Wood Box Fragment

A portion of a wood box with the name "REX BRAND" imprinted on it was recovered from Feature 2. This very likely comes from the Cudahy Packing Company, established in Milwaukee in the 1860s and producers of meat products, soap, and patent medicines under this brand name.

Domestic

Window Glass

A total of 1029 pieces of window glass were recovered in the excavations. All had a greenish tint and were patinized. Thickness varied between 1.5 and 3.0 mm, with about half (463 pieces) less than 2 mm in thickness. The largest percentage (60%) was recovered from Features 5-8.

Bottles

Bottle fragments totaled 545. Most of these were not identifiable, but some pertinent exceptions occurred. Of 37 bases, 24 bore embossed letters or symbols. In addition, 25 bottle necks were recovered, allowing some identification or estimates of dates of manufacture. Body fragments totaled 483, with a dozen having embossed information. A majority of these (275 pieces) were colorless and transparent. Colored fragments included green (109), amber (55), lavender (36), olive (8), and opaque black (1). We will first discuss embossed examples, then maker's marks on bottle bases, and finally bottle finishes (neck and lip, or rim).

Embossed bottles include several that are diagnostically important as chronological indicators. One is a fragment embossed (the "/"separates lines) with DR. PRICE'S/DELICIOUS/FLAVOR EXTRACTS (Figure 48h). This was a very popular product from the Price and Steele firm in Chicago, later the Price Flavoring Extract Company, manufactured between 1873 and early 1890s. This was found on the floor of Feature 1.

Several fragments from different bottles, when pieced together, identify DR. J.H. McLEAN'S/STRENGTHENING/CORDIAL/&/BLOOD PURIFIER (Figure 48a, i, j). These were manufactured in St. Louis and first advertised in 1865 and produced well into the 20th Century.[1] The locations of these included Trench C (fill), surface collection, and two locations in level one of Feature 9. One fragment of a rectangular bottle with indented and embossed panel reads CHAMBERLAIN'S/COLIC/CHOLERA/AND DIARRHOEA REMEDY (Figure 48l). This comes from Chamberlain and Company, DesMoines, Iowa. The embossed product was manufactured after 1892.[2] This was found in Feature 1 on the floor.

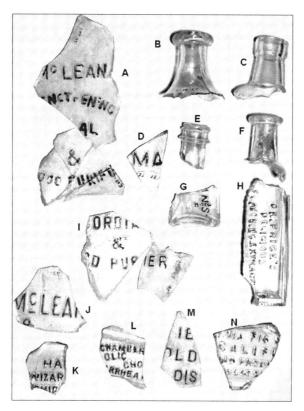

48. Embossed bottles.

A rectangular bottle side panel has the fragmentary embossed lines that, when unbroken, read CALIFORNIA FIG SYRUP CO./CALIF/STERLING PRODUCTS (INC)/SUCCESSOR (Figure 48n). This was manufactured from1878 into the 1880s, probably in San Francisco.[3] This one comes from Feature 9, at 10-20 cm.

One small flat side panel fragment bears embossed lines with the letters IE/OLD/DIS. This I interpret to be from a bottle of D[R]PIERCE'S/GOLDEN/MEDICAL DISCOVERY (Figure 48m). The Buffalo, N.Y. company introduced the product in 1870 and continued manufacture until about 1960.[4] This came from Trench A.

Other embossed fragments, including the script in Figure 49h, k, I am unable to identify, although one seems to represent a "Hair Wizard" product (Figure 48k). It is obvious from these datable bottles that only the final years of occupation are represented by this collection.

Bottle makers' marks[5] were common at the site. Three are illustrated here: In Figure 49d , a bottle base with embossed letters A.B.C.M around the perimeter following the mold seam, with an embossed "5" in the center. This is most likely Adolphus Busch Glass Manufacturing Company. There were plants at Belleville, IL (1886-c.1905) and St.Louis, MO (c.1891-1925). The fragment came from the general surface collection made in 1972. In Figure 49j, the letters A and B joined together, followed by "Co." represent the American Bottle Company, using this mark between 1905 and 1929. The center letter "B" with "110" below represent the bottle mold identification. This fragment came from Feature 7 just outside the east wall, near the surface. Finally, Figure 49l, with an "O" within a square was manufactured by the Owens Bottle Company, Toledo Ohio. Producing from 1903 to 1929, there is some inconclusive indication that this mark was first used in 1911 or later. It comes from the floor of Feature 1.

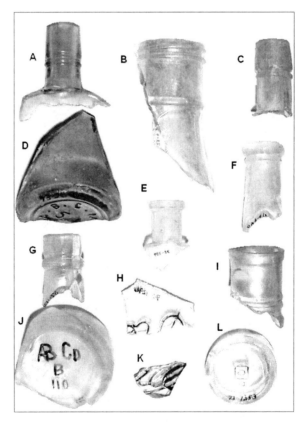

49. Bottle necks and bases

A bottle base with a "T" within an inverted triangle was manufactured by Turner Bros. Glass Co., Terre Haute, Indiana from about 1905 to 1930. It was found in Feature 1 fill, with no designated level. Another base, from a rectangular bottle, has an embossed diamond containing the letter "I". It was manufactured by the Illinois Glass Company, Alton, Illinois. The company produced from 1873 to 1929, but the company claimed, in its patent application, that the mark was first used in 1915. The fragment was recovered from the fill of Feature 1.

In addition to the maker's mark, each of our bases displays still another diagnostic feature: the mold seam (or lack thereof). A mold-made bottle leaves mold-seams where the parts of the mold meet, typically two halves of the bottle from side to side. A "hinge mold" runs from the neck, shoulder, and sides of the bottle through the base itself, so that a base fragment will show a mold seam which partially or completely bisects it. Such mold-made bottles date generally to 1875 or earlier. Obviously, the use of such bottles continues much later than their actual manufacture. None of our bottle bases have this feature. Instead, the base itself shows a mold seam around its outer circumference—at the "heel" of the bottle. Such bottles—made in a "cup base mold"—are later, generally, and can possibly date back to at least the 1870s (especially for drug and smaller bottles) though the majority date from the late 1880s to approximately 1915-1920—the effective end of the mouth-blown bottle era.

Finishes define how the bottle opening is constructed. All of our examples of collars and rims, or lips, indicate that these were not added to the neck as separate molten glass additions, but were rather hand-tooled modifications of the neck, having been re-heated after the mold-made bottle had sufficiently cooled. This is indicated by body seams (from the two-piece mold) extending up the neck and terminating short of—or just at—the collar or rim, but not extending into the latter. The collar and rim is then "tooled" by hand into its final shape.

Several of these are illustrated, and their differences have more stylistic or functional significance than chronological. Most could date any time after the 1870s. The common high collar with no separate lip is represented by the "brandy finish" (Figure 49a, c) with a tapered collar, and the "straight brandy" (Figure 49g) with a straight collar (a questionable distinction when gradations often unite the two in continuous variation). The "single collar" (Figure 49c) is similar, but has no bead-and-groove below the collar. The rounded "bead" rim,

Figure 48b, f) and the square variant (Figure 49e, i) are also common, the latter illustration having a tall collar with bead-and-groove base. Finally, the screw-cap finish (Figure 48e, Figure 49b) has external threads, commonly included in the mold itself, with the final lip hand-finished. These typically date later—most commonly after 1900.

The proveniences of these fragments are as follows: Figure 49a, Feature 4, surface; b, Feature 1, fill; c, Trench A, fill; e, Feature 4, level 1; f, Feature 9, level 2; I, Feature 12, adobe floor; and Figure 48b and e, Feature 1, 12 cm from floor; c, Feature 1, fill; f, Feature 9, 20-25 cm.

Collectively, these bottle data suggest a terminal date for the occupation/use of the St. Vrain's mill site. This also strongly suggests a broad use of the site after the turn of the century, rather than a focus on just some structures.

China

A total of 352 ceramic dinnerware fragments were recovered during excavations. These are itemized in Table 6. Most of these cannot be attributed to any time period, but a few have identifiable marks. Transfer patterns, such as that illustrated in Figure 50a (blue on white, Feature 9) and c (pink flower decal on two sides, Feature 2, 30-50 cm level) occurred on 41 pieces. Three had maker's marks on the exterior base.

Feature	White, plain	White, decorated	Non-white	Total
1	91	97	0	188
2	12	6	0	18
3	3	1	4	8
4	13	2	1	16
5	10	2	0	12
6	11	0	2	13
7	13	0	1	14
8	4	3	0	7
9	29	10	10	59
Tr A	10	0	0	10
Tr B	2	0	1	3
Tr C	2	0	0	2
Totals	**212**	**121**	**19**	**352**

Table 6. Ceramic distribution

The plate illustrated in Figure 50e bears the British royal coat of arms-the lion and the unicorn-with "Thomas Furnival & Sons" on the scroll above and "England" on the scroll below. It is an ironstone piece, and this particular design of the trade mark dates to about 1878-90.[6] It comes from Feature 6, 40-60 cm level. The small bowl illustrated in Figure 50b bears the same transfer print of the royal arms without the superior and inferior scrolls. Instead, the inscription above reads "Ironstone China" and, below, "Warranted", but with no discernible manufacturer's name. It was recovered from the floor of Feature 1. The cup in Figure 50d (Feature 1 fill) bears a rectangle with a sphinx figure resting on top. Within the rectangle are "Petrus/Regout Co./Maastricht" and "Made in Holland" below the rectangle. The Petrus Regout Company began manufacture in 1834 and adopted the sphinx trade mark in 1878.[7]

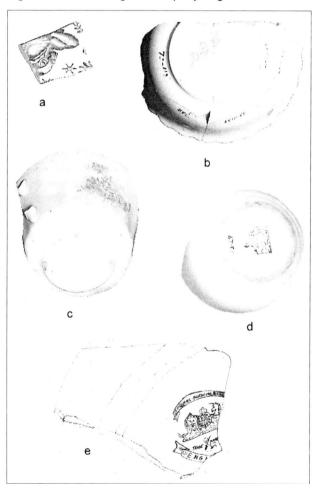

a

b

c

d

e

50. China

Clothing

The most common clothing items were buttons, but only 14 were recovered. Their distribution contributes no significant information as to room use.

Several interesting footware items were found. An iron shoe last for a child's shoe (general surface) is illustrated in Figure 51a, a child's shoe (b), the two-tone black and tan toe (c), and an adult shoe sole with peg fasteners (d). Hand driven wooden pegs were used in shoemaking to join sole and uppers throughout the U.S. until the early 19th Century. American machines using metal pins and clamping presses, about 1810, allowed mass production and replaced the more labor-intensive peg fasteners.[8] The pegs in our example (Figure 51d, photomicrograph 10x) appeared to be bone or wood, but an analysis by Roy Beavers, using a scanning electron microscope and energy dispersive x-ray analysis in the Earth Sciences Department, Southern Methodist University, identified these as zinc. Equally interesting is the pervasiveness of this technique at the turn of the century. Shoe pins supposedly replace pegs everywhere in the West after 1812, and nailing machines followed in 1829. A sewing machine was invented in 1858, and replaced earlier methods shortly afterward.[9]

Jewelry

A total of eight beads were found, all but two from Features 5, 7, and 8. Four were glass, one onyx, one turquoise, and one ceramic. A particularly interesting example is an elongated hexagonal glass bead, 3.6x20mm., recovered in Feature 9 (Figure 52d). A metal ring setting with faceted purple stone was recovered from Feature 5.

Ammunition

A total of eight shell casings were found during excavations. One of these, a .22 short cartridge, has an "H" headstamp. This "Henry" stamp identifies Remington ammunition that was manufactured from the late 1870s through 1939. Two .22 caliber rimfire cartridges, both short, date as early as the 1850s, while a centerfire .50-70 caliber copper casing with a Martin primer dates no earlier that its first use in the Model 1866 Springfield rifle. Information on these was provided by Dr. Robert Laury (personal communication, April 14, 2009).

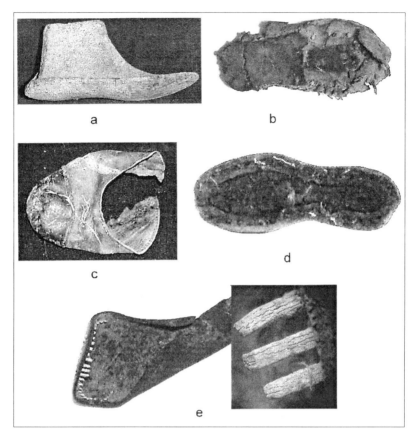

51. Footware

Wall Treatment

Interior walls of presumed residential structures were either wood-planked or adobe, and covered with a thick plaster. Onto this surface was commonly laid wallpaper, and fragments of both plaster and wallpaper survived in some abundance. The plaster was the very common *tierra blanca*—a native gypsum—reasonably abundant in the area and used by Hispanics in the area, then and now, as a finish on interior adobe walls. While a fragment of wallpaper was found in Feature 3 and in Feature 11, the vast majority was found in Features 5,

6, 7, and 8 in twelve separate locations. Most fragments were on *tierra blanca*. In one case, the plaster had been laid on wood; in another on adobe. Bright floral and other patterns in all colors are present.

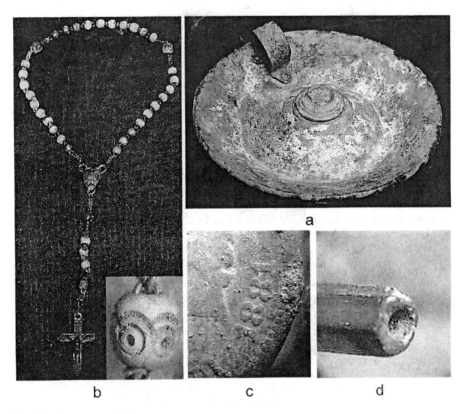

52. Miscellaneous artifacts

Miscellaneous Artifacts

Toys included two small lead wheels (Features 5 and 7), a marble (Feature 8), a rubberized doll's arm (Feature 9), and a tiny alabaster stature head (Feature 7). A rosary with copper crucifix and carved ivory beads (Figure 52b) was recovered from Feature 3, 20-40 cm. A penny with the date 1881 was found in Feature 5, level 1 (Figure 52c), and a tin candle holder, 12cm in diameter (Figure 52a), was found in Trench A.

9
Interpretations and Conclusions

Interpretations of the mill site are made complex by the knowledge that several owners made use of the facilities over the period between 1849 and 1901, and that structures were abandoned and created during this period. Contributing to the interpretations, however, are eyewitness accounts, historical documentation, and the archaeological investigations, and these help to inform us on the chronology of site use, functions of the structures, and shifts in the hydrologic power system.

The Chronology of Site Use

Documentary evidence is abundant in confirming the construction and initial use of the mill by Ceran St. Vrain. Constructed in 1849, but not provisioned with milling machinery until the following year, the millroom and contiguous structures (Features 1, 2, and probably 3) caught fire during the night of July 28, 1864, as discussed in Chapter 3. During this first occupation, the preponderance of wheat grown in Taos valley was processed into flour here, and both wheat, bran, and corn were warehoused here.

While Jacob Beard was his miller and millright at Mora, and was undoubtedly the millright in charge of laying out the Taos mill, we do not know who the miller was in Taos. The 1850 Taos census fails to identify a "miller".

Ceran may have operated a sawmill on the premises in the 1850s. He certainly acquired experience in this growing industry, establishing a sawmill in Mora County in the following decade.

Ceran's third entrepreneurial venture, distilling, was also possibly conducted at the mill site by 1854, when the Burgwin commanding officer visited the mill to sample its spirituous liquors (see Chapter 3, note 25). Unfortunately subsequent operations at the mill site combined with scavenging of usable remains by locals prevented any archaeological evidence for sawmill or distillery. It is known that both industries were conducted along this river in several locations during the 1800s.

After its destruction by fire in 1864, it was abandoned for an unknown period. By this time, extensive operations in Mora and in southern Colorado Territory made it infeasible to rebuild the mill structure, although outlying buildings remained intact. It is possible that Ceran leased the property prior to eventually selling, but few records remain. Curiously, a crudely carved cornerstone found at the site during excavations bears the date "5/7/92" and the cryptic initials "JCM".

The next known period of occupation and use is at the turn of the century, from the late 1800s to final abandonment in about 1901. It is this use for which eyewitness accounts and the archaeological record are most informative. Sr. Appolonio Sanchez recalled visiting the site in 1901, when a "small gristmill" was running, utilizing rebuilt Features 1 and 2. These, and Features 3 and 4, according to him, had stone foundations and adobe walls. At that time, Features 10-13 stood as adobe buildings with flat roofs, and he recalls that the waterwheel was horizontal. Sr. Sanchez could not recall having seen Features 5-8. The fact that they were some distance away from the milling operation, and probably non-descript, could account for this lapse, as the archaeological evidence certainly places them on site by the turn of the century. He also recalled seeing the wooden sluiceway, but, regardless of the type of wheel, the sluice must have been repositioned at that time, and probably did not utilize the same diversion of the stream on the western perimeter of the site.

Both Sanchez and Sr. Jacob Bernal, of Ranchos, confirmed that the site was abandoned by 1903. Sr. Sanchez recalls regular trips down the highway past the mill site in the early 1900s, and claims that the site appeared to be abandoned after 1901. Sr. Bernal visited the site in 1911, when the site lay in ruins, and also claimed that milling operations ceased sometime during 1901. Sr. Sanchez further observed that, in the years postdating his 1901 visit, adobe bricks and vigas were systematically scavenged by the local population.

On the matter of a possible sawmill operation at the site, Mr. Sanchez claimed that a sawmill did exist some distance upstream, but not at the mill site. This could possibly refer to continued use of the sawmill utilized by Cantonment Burgwin in 1852-53.

It is significant that the identified embossed bottles recovered from Feature 1, as well as from other locations, consistently point to use during the last three decades of the 19th century. Confounding the end-date chronology are four bottle bases—three in Feature 1—that bear maker's marks purportedly in use only *after* 1903. Of course, occasional later contamination of an abandoned site by visitors would not be unexpected.

Hearsay evidence suggests that Frank Trambley bought and operated the site during this last period—from about 1891 until 1901—but no evidence to support this has been found. It is likely that this ownership and operation is confused with Trambley's purchase of Ceran's stone mill in Mora.

After its penultimate ownership, the land in most of the valley, including the site, was purchased in 1908 by the Santa Barbara Tie and Pole Company. In a land-for-timber trade, the U.S. Forest Service later acquired the land as part of the Carson National Forest, under whose protection it remains today.

It appears likely, therefore, that the original mill consisted of earlier structures built on the excavated stone foundations of Features 1-3. It is also probable that this was solely a day-labor site which required no fulltime residence. That the miller was sleeping in the milling room when the fire broke out confirms this. Hence, no separate structures for residence were likely to have been part of the complex.

The additional buildings represented by Features 4 and 10-13 appear to have been part of a single construction episode, using different materials and techniques. While the archaeology gives little insight into their function, their location would have interrupted the hydrologic apparatus for powering an overshot wheel, and so they must coincide with the last phase of occupation.

The chronological position of Features 5-8 most certainly include the most recent period. This is readily confirmed by the 1881 Indian head penny in Feature 5 and the china fragment from Feature 6 with maker's mark dating it to post-1878.

Functions of the Structures

Architecture, profiles, and fill content together support the use of Features 1-3 in primary milling operations during both phases of occupation. Feature 1 could only have been the primary flour processing room, most likely three floors: the lower floor for the pit wheel, bridge tree, and spindle with pinion/stone nut; the stone floor housing the runner and bedder stones in their vat, with the hopper above; and the bin floor or loft where the grain bin was located and where wheat sacks would have been hoisted for storage pending grinding. It was apparently on the stone floor where the 1864 fire broke out, from an untended candle on the window near the stones. The meal trough and bin, and sacking operation for the flour, might have been on a separate second floor, or on the pit floor.

Feature 2 would logically have served as warehousing for ground flour and meal. The thick layer of charcoal and ash perhaps marks the end of the St. Vrain operation, with the compact earth above reflecting the later occupation.

Feature 3 had only a single occupational level in the fill, and may well have been a store room for tools and spare parts as well as a repair shop for wood frames, leather belts, and other milling components. The abundance of wood scrap found here, and in the adjacent Feature 4, also suggests the possibility of a sawmill operation in this location.

As previously discussed, Feature 4 was apparently an open courtyard, lacking a definitive wall on the north (arroyo) side. An open work area consistent with sawmill or blacksmith operations is suggested. Recovered material culture in this feature included horseshoes, nails, a broken drill bit, a horse's hoof, and assorted metal scrap.

These building arrangements, however, would have been logistically awkward since the access road was on the west, or mountain, side of the operation while the milling was done on the east side adjacent to the river. Loading and unloading operations were thus separated from the rooms receiving grain and supplying finished products.

The artifactual and architectural evidence strongly supports a domiciliary function for Features 5-8. The discovery of an undamaged pit-wheel gear section in Feature 6 further confirms that this building complex was in use during commercial milling operations. Artifactual evidence, however, confirms use of these facilities at the turn of the century. It remains possible, of course, that earlier versions of these features were also present during Ceran's milling operation, but no evidence specifically supports this.

Changes in the Hydrology of the Mill

Sr. Sanchez' recollection that the mill wheel was horizontal when he visited the site in 1901 demands serious consideration. That this recollection is probably accurate is supported by Sanchez' description of Features 10-13. Feature 10, at least, could not have existed contemporaneously with the headrace and sluiceway which fed the original overshot wheel.

A horizontal wheel would either have been one of the Leffel turbine wheels, popular at the time, or simply a reversion to the horizontal wooden wheels common to the many private grist mills in the area. It most likely was the former. Mr. Sanchez did not suggest that the mill was a small-scale enterprise, and the necessary shift in hydrology would have required a relatively significant construction effort.

This latter requirement, of course, draws our attention to the complexity of stone, wood beam, and posthole alignments characterizing Trench A. The substantial but ambiguous cultural refuse recovered from this area, and the intervening dissection into the site contour between this and the retaining wall east and north of Feature 9, characterize this as having an important function. Substantial activity was focused here, and it is tempting to suggest that the Trench A area was altered and stone reinforced to provide a new channel for the river in driving a turbine wheel from the side rather than a vertical wheel from the top. Such alteration would have been necessary, probably in the form of a short stream diversion, at about this point.

It is unfortunate that excavations did not proceed further in this area in 1973. Excavations in subsequent years were under the supervision of a different Field School Director who focused on prehistoric archaeology, as I took on responsibilities as Associate Director of the Fort Burgwin Research Center, under Fred Wendorf, in the fall of that year through summer, 1975, and continued as Director of the Center from 1975 through 1977.

It is important to recognize that the recovered mill machinery, particularly the iron gear fragments, almost certainly relate to this most recent period of operation. With final abandonment early in the 20th century, it is probable that other millers in the Taos or Mora area acquired any usable equipment and machinery. It was no doubt fortuitous for archaeology that the succeeding ownership by Santa Barbara removed the site from potential homesteading, and that the subsequent stewardship by the Carson National Forest both protected the site and made it available, by permit, for our excavation.

List of Illustrations

Fronticepiece: Ceran St. Vrain, copy of a photo given to his daughter, Felicitas.

1. Geneaology of the St. Vrain family.
2. Ceran St. Vrain in 1860.
3. Charles Bent.
4. William Bent.
5. Marcellin St. Vrain.
6. Royal Red ("Rel"), sister of Chief Red Cloud and first wife of Marcellin St. Vrain.
7. Mary Louise St. Vrain, youngest child of Marcellin and Rel.
8. Map of New Mexico and Colorado, showing early military and civilian forts.
9. Lucien Maxwell.
10. Charles Beaubien.
11. General Sterling Price.
12. Col. E. V. Sumner.
13. Joseph Hersch.
14. Grain production, Taos and Mora Counties.
15. Location of the Taos mill on the Rio Grande del Rancho.
16. Location of the stone mill at Mora.
17. Louisa Branch, Ceran's third wife.
18. Ceran's house in Mora.
19. Early photograph of Ceran's stone mill.
20. John M. Francisco.
21. Hiram Vasquez.
22. Felicitas St. Vrain, daughter of Ceran and Louisa Branch.
23. Macario Gallegos.
24. Wedding photograph of Macario Gallegos and Felicitas St. Vrain Gallegos.
25. Benedict St. Vrain and wife, Martha Longuevan, possibly a wedding photo.
26. St. Vrain's stone mill in Mora in the early 20th century.
27. Early drawing of a private grist mill.
28. Schematic diagram of a typical 19th century commercial flour mill, inside view.
29. Schematic diagram of a typical 19th century commercial flour mill, showing millwheel.
30. Ceran's stone mill at Mora today.
31. Detail view of iron wheel and wheel pit at the Mora mill.
32. Map of TA 600, St. Vrain's Mill.

33. Students conducting initial surface survey, view from west.
34. TA 600 before excavation. View from terrace east of Highway 3 (foreground). Arrow indicates 19th Century road west of site.
35. The Rio Grande del Rancho in June, 1973. Taken where tailrace would have re-entered.
36. Plan and profile, Features 1-3.
37. View north into arroyo from Feature 3, before excavation.
38. Plan and profiles, Features 5-8.
39. Feature 6 walls before excavation.
40. Plan of Features 4, 10-13.
41. Trench A (extension).
42. Plan of Trench A plus extension.
43. Profile, west wall of Trench A.
44. Profiles, Trenches B and C.
45. Profiles, Trenches D and E.
46. Mechanical iron artifacts.
47. Leather drive belt fragments.
48. Embossed bottles.
49. Bottle necks and bases.
50. China.
51. Footware.
52. Miscellaneous artifacts.

List of Tables

Table 1. Agriculture in Colorado and New Mexico in the 19th Century.
Table 2. Cost and income valuation, flour production.
Table 3. Grain and flour contracts for the Navajo, 1864.
Table 4. Cut nail distribution.
Table 5. Wire nail distribution.
Table 6. Ceramic distribution.

Notes

Preface and Acknowledgments

1. Wetherington, Ronald K. (2006), 401.
2. This information comes from a letter written by Benedict Marcellin St. Vrain's second wife, Martha Longuevan, in 1909. Referenced in the archival guide to the Delassus-St. Vrain Family Collection, Missouri Historical Society. See www.mohistory.org/files/archives_ guides/DelassusCollection.pdf.

Chapter 1: St. Vrain and his New Mexico Connections

1. Dictionary of American Biography (1935), Vol. XVI. His birth is listed as 1798 in the Delassus-St. Vrain Family Collection, Missouri Historical Society, St. Louis, but the geneology therein disagrees with other sources on several names and dates. Likewise inconsistent is the online Earl Fischer Database of St. Louisians, St. Louis Genaeological Society. Christine St. Vrain, the gr-gr-gr-gr granddaughter of Ceran's younger brother Domatille, has traced the entire genealogy intensively, and has generously provided her results. Where other records disagree, I rely on her judgment. The following genealogical discussion is taken from these sources, and the dates and names used herein are deemed most accurate, but may not be.
2. Weber (1995), 258-269. Odille's father, Major Phillipe François Camille deHault Delassus, was Ceran's father's eldest brother.
3. Ceran had lived with the Prattes after the death of his father in 1818. Weber (1971), 89-90.
4. Papers of the St. Louis Fur Trade, Frame 537. Etienne Provost and partner François Leclerc were among the earliest trappers to appear in New Mexico territory to exploit the beaver colonies in the streams from Taos to southern Colorado. They were in Taos at least as early as 1823 and played a prominent role in the highly competitive trade in subsequent years; Weber (1971), 49.
5. Papers of the St. Louis Fur Trade, Frame 599.
6. Lavender (1972), 139; Dunham (1982), 146-165.
7. Dunham, Ibid.,148.
8. Baillio had been in the Indian trade at Fort Osage with George Sibley in 1820-22, had formed a partnership with him and Lilburn Boggs in 1822, buying and selling government supplies, and in the following year had established a trading post with William "Old Bill" Williams on the Neosho River (a tributary of the Arkansas in eastern Kansas). Baillio entered the Santa Fe trade in 1823 or 1824 and was in Santa Fe the year he partnered with St. Vrain; Weber (1971), 101.
9. Young, a carpenter from Tennessee seeking his fortune on the frontier, with Kentuckian William Wolfskill, had come to New Mexico with William Becknell on his second trip across the pristine Santa Fe Trail. The train—three wagons—traveled in the late summer of 1822 with a group of twenty-one men. Weber (1971), 58.
10. Dunham (1982), 150, cites the date as Nov. 29, 1826; Lavender (1971), 70, and Weber (1971), 113, as Aug. 29.

11. Marshall (1916),19:2. "S.W." was "Old Bill" Williams, one of the early traders and trappers in the Rocky Mountains and an interpreter for the George C. Sibley surveying expedition, first arrived in Taos in late fall of 1825, from where he trapped until 1834. Voelker (1995).

12. Dunham (1982), 150-152; Weber (1971), 171f. He had apparently missed the birth of his first son, Vincent, on May 10, 1827.

13. An unsupported explanation is that Pratte was bitten by a rabid dog. Dunham, Ibid.,151.

14. Weber (1971), 171.

15. "No. 17. On 30 September a passport was issued to the citizen of the United States N.A. Ceran Sambrans to enter the states of Chihuahua and Sonora on commercial business" New Mexico Passport Records, Santa Fe 1827-1828, Manuscript Collection 184, Folder 1, Center for Southwestern Research, Zimmerman Library, U. of New Mexico. St. Vrain continued trade with Mexico for several years thereafter: On March 8, 1832 "a passport was issued to the foreigner Santiago C.M. Halliday to the states of Chihuahua and Sonora for commercial business for the naturalized citizen, Ceran Sambrano" Ibid. References provided by Christine St. Vrain.

16. Cited in Hanosh (1967), 74. Hanosh believes this Lavoise Ruel could be Joseph Rouelle, an early French settler in Mora, who later had business dealings with Ceran. Dunham (1982) 153, calls him "Savase Ruel".

17. Cited in Parish (1961), 5.

18. Dunham (1982), 153.

19. Barreiro (1967), 286-7, my translation. The English version, p. 108, translates "queman sus archetas" as "burn their merchandise", which is confusing.

20. Barreiro, Ibid, 108.

21. Mumey (1956), 15-16.

22. Lavender (1972), 154; Lecompte (1978), 17.

23. Weber (1971), 64.

24. Lavender (1972), 139-154. First called the "New Fort William", it soon earned the iconic name Bent's Fort.

25. Dunham (1982), 155.

26. Stevens (1993), 169-171; New Galenian, May 30, 1832.

27. Lavender (1982), 154; Weber (1971), 211.

28. Carter (1995). Carter, and the author, also consulted the "Early Far West Notebook" series of the Francis W. Cragin Papers, originals in The Pioneer's Museum, Colorado Springs. The author used copies made by Janet Lecompte, which she donated with other documents to the DeGolyer Library, Southern Methodist University. References to the Cragin Collection herein come from this latter source.

29. Lavender (1982), 189-199.

30. For an excellent account of this episode and its causes, see Weber (1982), Ch. 12.

31. Hafen (1952).

32. Cragin Collection, Notebook IV, p. 29-30. While Carter and others, including Mary herself, place her birth date as 1848, her brother Charles told Cragin she was born on March 10, 1846 and "and is only two years younger than he."

33. Lavender (1982), 332f; 442 n.9.

34. Sopris (1945); Cragin Collection, Notebook IX, p. 23.

35. Alois Scheurich, as told to F.W. Cragin, Cragin Collection, Early Far West Notebook XII, p 64.

36. For excellent discussions of the Las Animas Grant, see Van Ness, John R. & Christine M. (1980).

37. Anonymous, "The Charles Bent Papers," *NMHR* 31(1956): 163-164.

38. Ibid., 163.

39. Baker and Harrison (1986), 13-14. Major C.F. Ruff described the structure in 1860, where he camped while on an Indian campaign; see Kenner, Charles L. (1969), 132, n.61. The post had a very brief life due to threats from hostile tribes.

40. Murphy (1983). Murphy, p.27, states that St. Vrain's sister had married a Menard, but I find no evidence for this. The Chouteaus and Menards, however, shared several cousin marriages.

41. Lavender (1972), 219f. Between marriages, the grieving and lonely Kit had proffered interest in Marie Felicité St. Vrain, sixteen year old visiting daughter of Ceran's dead brother, Felix Auguste. After all, Adaline needed a woman's supervision. Ceran sent Marie Felicité quickly back to St. Louis.

42. Roberts (2000), 32f.

43. For accounts of the Taos Rebellion and aftermath from eyewitnesses, see McNierney (1980).

44. Price, Sterling, "Report by Colonel Sterling Price to the Adjutant General, 15 February 1847," in McNierney (1980), 45f.

45. McNierney (1980), 49f.

46. Lavender (1972), 326.

47. Dunham (1982), 162; Lavender (1972), 322.

48. Lavender (1972), 326.

49. William C. Carr Papers. Dorcas, born in 1807, was the 5th of 10 children of Silas Bent and Martha Kerr. Charles was the oldest (b. 1799) and her brother Silas was the youngest (b. 1820). Earl Fischer Database.

50. Dunham (1982), 159; *House Journal, Aug 7, 1848*, 30 Cong. 1 sess.

51. Lavender (1972), 338.

52. Dunham (1982), 164. He defeated Miguel Antonio Otero, *New York Times*, June 29, 1859, p.3, reporting from the St. Louis Republican.

53. Garrard (1955), 15.

54. One source claims his resignation was due to ill-health from being overweight. Monnett (1996), 49.

55. Dunham (1982), 165, claims that Ceran moved permanently to Mora in 1855, but we have records of Ceran's commercial business, deed transactions, and official activities in the Taos Masonic lodge during much of the 1860s. Ceran's son Felix told F.W. Cragin that Ceran never actually lived in Mora as his home, but always in Taos. He had a house and store in Mora, however, and spent a good deal of time there. Cragin Collection, Notebook VI, p. 11.

56. *Rocky Mountain News*, Vol XI, November 1, 1870, p.1, c.4.

57. While there is little controversy over Ceran's first and last unions and the two children produced therefrom, there is considerable disagreement over the second. Lavender (1972), 231;427 n.10, claims that this "wife" was the eldest daughter of Charles Beaubien, although noting that "almost nothing is known" about this marriage. His source is Frémont's account of his second expedition. Francis Cragin, however, from an interview with José Felix St. Vrain in 1907, lists the husbands of all five Beaubien daughters and Ceran is not one of them. Lavender further claims that Louisa Branch was Ceran's second wife. Cragin, citing Jesse Nelson, states that Ceran "lived with Vicente's mother, later with Ignacia Trujillo; later with Pabla Trujillo; then with her daughter Luisa Branch" (Cragin Collection, Notebook

VIII). Felix told Cragin that his mother was Maria Trujillo and that "Vicente's mother was a Mexican woman whose maiden name was Luna" (Notebook VI).

Chapter 2. Flour, Mercantilism, and the Territorial Economy

1. Frazer (1983), 7.
2. Ibid. 28.
3. Ball (2001), *xxx*.
4. Frazer (1983), 40.
5. Bowen to Sumner, December, 1852, *Register of Letters Received, and Letters Received by Headquarters, Ninth Military Department, 1848-1853*, Records of the U.S. Army Continental Commands, 1821-1920, Microcopy 1102, Record Group 393, National Archives, Washington, D.C. [hereafter, LR, RG number, NA].
6. In 1853, for example, the subsistence estimate in the Department for a year, including bacon, ham, rice, coffee and sugar, was 287,000 lbs, while flour contracts totaled 600,000 lb. Bowen to Sumner, Ibid; Frazer (1972), 225.
7. Gordon to McFerrin, May 5, 1852, LR, RG 393, NA .
8. Frazer (1972), 214.
9. Simeon Hart was a New York native who was stationed in El Paso as a member of the Missouri Mounted Volunteers during the Mexican War. With Sterling Price's occupation of Santa Cruz de Rosales in Chihuahua, he met and married Jesusita Siqueiros. Her father, Leonardo, owned a gristmill there, stimulating Hart's interest in flour milling. He built his own in El Paso in 1849, where he lived for the remainder of his life. His many flour contracts with the army were frequently filled in large part with flour from the Siqueiros mill in Santa Cruz. Frazer (1972), 220-221.
10. Frazer (1983), 102.
11. St. Vrain to Sumner, October 14, 1851, LR, RG 393, NA..
12. Frazer (1968), 134.
13. St. Vrain to Sumner, October 14, 1851, LR, RG 393, NA.
14. Sumner to St. Vrain, October 17, 1851, *Letters Sent by the Ninth Military Department, Department of New Mexico, and the District of New Mexico, 1849-1890*, Microcopy 1072, [hereafter LS, RG 393, NA.]
15. Gordon to McFerrin, May 5, 1852,LR, RG 393, NA.
16. McFerrin to Gordon, May 12, 1852, LS, RG 393, NA. Fort Massachusetts was constructed in the fall of 1852 and quarters were occupied by early October.
17. Jackson to Sumner, October 1, 1852, LR, RG 393, NA.
18. Ransom to Sumner, November 15, 1852, LS, RG 393, NA.
19. Sturgis to Ransom, December 11, 1852, LS, RG 393, NA.
20. Sumner to Blake, December 11, 1852, LS, RG 393, NA.
21. Blake to Sumner, December 24, 1852, LR, RG 393, NA.
22. Elder and Weber (1996), 148.
23. Miller (1989), 33.
24. Frazer (1972), 215-16.
25. Isaac McCarty, born in 1812 in Missouri (possibly Westport) was one of a long line of McCartys in that region. He died in Taos in October, 1850. This must have been immediately after

arriving from Santa Fe, for he resided in a large household there during the 1850 census, enumerated along with a Wm. McCrarty, Lucian Stewart, both Ceran and Vincent St. Vrain, and two servants (Federal Census, Santa Fe, Schedule I, 1850, Household #1211). After McCarty's death, St. Vrain established an association—if not a partnership—with Robert Cary, who became his agent for negotiating sales of corn and wheat (see Jackson to Sumner, October 1, 1852, LR, RG 393, NA).

26. Frazer (1972), 221-2, 229, 230.

27. Ibid., 221.

28. Ibid., 225-6.

29. Sumner to Bowen, April 9, 1852, LS, RG 393, NA.

30. Frazer (1972), 226.

31. The mill, together with a distillery, brewery, "and all other buildings" was located "on the south side of the Rio Chiquito about a half mile above the Plaza of the City of Santa Fe,..." Deed Record, Santa Fe County, Book A, p 13, New Mexico State Records Center and Archives, Santa Fe [hereafter SRCA].

32. Today this is the Randall Davey House, home of the New Mexico Ornithological Society. The mill will be discussed in the following chapter.

33. Miller (1989), 369.

34. These and the following data come from the 7th Census of the United States, 1850, Table XI: Agriculture, and from the 8th Census, Agriculture in the United States in 1860, pp. 178-9, Bureau of the Census, 1864. Some of these quantities inexplicably differ from Frazer (1983), 186, citing the same census sources.

35. Ball (2001), xxx; Frazer (1983), 185f.

36. See Beck and Haase (1969).

37. Cited in Callon (1962), 31.

38. 8th Census of the U.S.: Manufactures by Counties, Territory of New Mexico, p. 666; by contrast, distilling and sawmilling, the other two uses to which grist mills were frequently put, yielded $3,720 and $700, respectively, net of expenses, excluding capital investment of $39,000 and $2,000.

39. Santa Fe Gazette, October 20, 1860.

40. Frazer (1983), 180. Dold owned a grist mill after 1870.

41. Frazer (1972), 230.

42. Parish (1961), 70.

43. Miller (1989), 6.

44. Ltr., Lt. Col. William Chapman to Maj. Baca, Nov. 7, 1861, Arrott Collection, Vol. 8, p. 133.

45. Arrott Collection, vol. 10, p. 82.

46. Carleton to Garrison, August 14, 1862, LS, RG 393, NA.

47. Condition of the Indian Tribes (1865), 223-279.

48. Carleton to St. Vrain, April 13, 1864, LS, RG 393, NA.

49. Andres Dodd was Andrew Dold, who with his brother John were merchants and bankers in Las Vegas, New Mexico—each had his own business on opposite corners of the plaza but did business in partnership as well—and sent wheat that they purchased to St.Vrain's Mora mill for processing into flour, when they did not provide unprocessed wheat directly to the government. They also provided almost 500,000 pounds of flour to the government during 1860-61 (Frazer 1972, 228). The Dold brothers, whose name was variously spelled Dodd and Dole (see, e.g., Kingsbury to Webb, October 1, 1859, in Elder and Weber (1996),181),

conducted business with several firms, including Webb and Kingsbury, in at least one case selling land warrants to them for resale in the east (Ibid., 54).

50. Maxwell constructed a large, but crudely built, stone flour mill at his ranch and settlement in Rayado (now Cimarron), the "Aztec Mill", in 1864. The Rocky Mountain News reported, on August 31, 1864, "L.B. Maxwell, of the celebrated Cimarron Ranch, is erecting a steam grist mill at Rayado, that will turn out 300 barrels of flour per day", *Weekly Rocky Mountain News*, August 31, 1864, p.3, c. 2. It was the second steam mill in the territory; Hersch's Santa Fe mill was the first such to be built, in 1858, (Frazer 1983, 106-7). Interestingly, Fierman (1984), 183, n.36, claims that Alexander Gusdorf built the first such mill in New Mexico, in 1880, in Ranchos de Taos. The Gusdorf mill is discussed further in Chapter 5.

51. Callon (1962), 43-4. The army in 1852 fixed a fanega of grain at 140 lbs., according to Frazer (1983), 195, n.14. Either the standard changed by the 1860s, or it varied by quality of grain, or Callon is in error.

52. Miller (1989), 369.

53. Frazer (1968), 122.

54. Ibid., 141.

55. Frazer (1983), 45.

56. Frazer (1968), 169; Frazer (1954), 62.

57. Frazer (1983), 107.

58. Ceran St.Vrain had died the previous year and Vincent had continued flour production in Mora.

59. The Romero Mill, south of Mora at La Cueva, was built in 1860 and supplied flour to Fort Union and other military posts. The mill still stands, as a designated Historic Site.

60. Nash to A.A.A. General, District of New Mexico, Arrott Collection, vol. 25, p. 142.

61. Fraser (1972), 214.

62. Risch (1989), 304.

63. Carleton to St. Vrain, April 13, 1864, LS, RG 98, NA..

64. Parish (1961), 72.

65. Ibid, 74.

66. Albert Gallatin Boone, grandson of Daniel Boone, was born in 1806 in Kentucky and moved with his family to Missouri. He worked for Lilburn Boggs at the Fort Osage Trading Post, and in 1838 established his own trading post at Westport. He later became a business associate of William Bent.

67. St. Vrain to Francisco, April 29, 1861, Daniel W. Working Papers.

68. Boone had merchant stores in Westport and Council Groves, as well as Denver. In an interview with Mrs. Ben Spencer in 1903, C.F. Cragin was told that Boone quit his business, "having failed at Westport," and that in the spring of 1860, Boone "came to Denver to take charge of Col. Ceran St. Vrain's Denver store." (Cragin Collection, Notebook XXIII, p 23.)

69. This is quite possibly Tancrede Mignault (in some documents Tancre de Mignault), who would have been about 23 years old at that time. Theodore Mignault, a longer term associate and sometime partner of Ceran, who indeed operated his store in Taos for awhile, was 37 in 1861—hardly a "young Mignault", notwithstanding Ceran's 59 years.

70. Daigre to Francisco, January 20, 1864, Daniel W. Working Papers. Daigre, Francisco, and other Colorado merchants and ranchers mentioned here will be discussed more fully in Chapter 4.

71. *Daily Rocky Mountain News*, August 29, 1860 and September 5, 1850, respectively.

72. *Las Animas Leader*, May 23, 1873, p. 3, c. 1. In the previous decade butter was generally purchased in Missouri and freighted west. See, e.g., Elder and Weber (1996), 142.

73. Daigre to Francisco, Daniel W. Working Papers; Baxter (1987), 28-29; Parish (1961), 153.

74. For an excellent discussion of the early sheep trade see Baxter (1987), especially 137-150.

75. Baxter, Ibid., 149.

76. St. Vrain to Francisco, April 29, 1861, Daniel W. Working Papers,

77. Daigre to Francisco, May 2, 1864, Daniel W. Working Papers. Los Pinos was a ranch leased by the army in 1862 and used briefly as a supply depot. It was just south of Albuquerque. See Miller (1987).

Chapter 3. St. Vrain's First Mills: Taos and Mora

1. St. Vrain received at least two mail contracts in the winter and spring of 1849; Taylor (1971), 25.

2. Garrard (1955), 168; 170.

3. The true French buhr (burr) was a hard, silicious granite, heavy in quartz and extremely dense, ideal for millstone use because of its durability and fine grain. Quarried in La Ferte-sous-Fauarre, near Paris, and shipped (as ballast) to the United States, the stones were very expensive. A set of two would weigh a ton or more. For an interesting background, see Watts (2002).

4. Francis W. Cragin, interview with Jacob Beard, Oct. 31, 1904, Cragin Collection, Notebook, II, p.23.

5. The location is described as a tract of land "with a house thereon at present occupied by Said St Vrain as a Store house situated in the Town of San Francisco del Rancho in Said County and bounded on the north by the Main Street of Said Town." Taos County Records, Deeds, 1853-1869, Book A-1, 163, 27 January 1858, SRCA.

6. A methodical reconnaissance by Charles Hawk of Taos, personal communication, indicates that the road to Taos crossed to the west of the river just upstream at an elevation of approximately 7,220 ft.-a likely spot for the stream itself to have been diverted to feed the forebay. The river at the mill runs next to a U.S.G.S. benchmark of 7,155 ft.

7. See Baxter (1990), Introducton, Ch. V.

8. Ransom to Sturgis, January 21, 1853, LR, RG393, NA. Asa Estes was a mountaineer and early associate of Bent and St. Vrain. He was a tavern keeper in Taos where, the evening of the Taos Rebellion of 1847, the insurgents had fortified their courage with whiskey. Robert Carey was a merchant from Delaware listed in the 1850 Taos Census as thirty-five years of age. During the 1850s Carey was an agent for, if not a partner of, St. Vrain. Carey and Estes had sold the sawmill to Josiah Webb, who gave Ransom permission to use it, "provided I will put it in order." (Ransom to Sumner, October 24, 1852, LR, Ibid.) Carey had borrowed money from the Messervy & Webb firm in the mid-fifties and paid it off in 1859, after he was awarded the sutlership at Cantonment Burgwin (Elder and Weber, 1996, 147).

9. Bloom (1927). This "brandy still" was located on the Rio Grande del Rancho west of Ranchos de Taos, probably close to the plaza of Las Cordovas, just over two miles northwest of Ranchos along current Highway 240—the common route into Taos during that time.

10. Garrard (1955), 166. Writers have often assumed that the "Taos canyon" through which Garrard passed was the one further north, from Angel Fire, and this also had a distillery at the time. Garrard's description, however, leaves little doubt that his reference and his trail was down the Rio Grande del Rancho.

11. Lecompte, (n.d.), p. 1.

12. Frazer (1972), p, 219.

13. Frazer (1968), 134, 140.

14. Bloom (1942) 125. The correct spelling of the last name is Reed.

15. Cragin Collection, Notebook II, p. 23.

16. Grier to McLaws, June 6, 1850, LR, RG393, NA.

17. Gordon to McFerran, May 16, 1852, LR, RG393, NA.

18. Adams to Sykes, September 8, 1853, LR, RG393, NA.

19. Bennett (1996), 41.

20. Abel (1915), 357-358.

21. Sumner to Ransom, August 10, 1852, LS, RG393; Sumner to Ransom, August 24, 1852, Ibid.

22. Sumner to Bowen, Nov. 7, 1852, LS, RG 393, NA. Inexplicably, Frazer ("Purveyors," 224-5) lists the Albuquerque portion as 7/20 and states that "6/20 of the flour was not accounted for in Sumner's instructions."

23. Sumner to Bowen, Ibid.

24. Fraser (1972), 225.

25. Taos County Records, Deeds, 1853-1869, SRCA, 160-165. In addition, St. Vrain probably operated a distillery on the premises. In March of 1854, Maj. George Blake, commander of nearby Cantonment Burgwin, visited the establishment to sample its wares. Will Gorenfeld, "The Battle of Cieneguilla: the Historical Record," in press.

26. St. Vrain and Mignault to Francisco, August 17, 1864. Working Papers. Mignault wrote the letter; Weekly Rocky Mountain News, August 31, 1864, p.3, c. 2.

27. Beard was born in 1828 in Virginia, but apprenticed as a miller in St. Louis. He was probably a millwright as well, and it is likely that he helped complete the Mora mill. By his account, he worked there through the winter of 1852, when he left for California in search of his fortune in gold. F.W. Cragin interview, Oct. 31, 1904, Cragin Collection, Notebook II, p.24.

28. The enigmatic Mignault is one of two with whom St. Vrain had long-term connections. Theodore Mignault, born in Quebec in 1824, lived in Taos as early as 1849, managed the merchant store in Taos, and was involved in several of Ceran's enterprises in Mora and Colorado. He is listed in the 1860 Taos Census as being 39 years old. He was living in Ceran's household in Mora when Ceran died, and was co-administrator of his estate. The younger Tancrede Mignault appears in Taos records in 1860 and 1861 as witness to probate transactions. His relation to Theodore, if any, is not apparent, although it is likely that they are related. A Tancrede Mignault is listed in the 1881 Canadian census as a merchant living in Quebec and born in 1837. In the 1901 Census his birth date is given as 1834.

29. Lecompte (N.D.), 2, citing Beard's "Reminiscences".

30. This is one of several tracts of land, including the mill, mortgaged to Joseph Pley by St. Vrain in late January, 1858, Taos County Records, Deeds, 1853-1869, Book A-1, SRCA, 157-165.

31. Carson (1964). In a footnote, Carson suggests that the reference was to Vincent St. Vrain, since he was then a resident of Mora, but this was Ceran's mill, which Vincent managed.

32. Frazer (1954), 36; Bennett (1996), 41.

33. Miller (1997), 47.

34. The following data are from Taos County Records, Deeds. 1853-1869. Serial 16701, Book A-1, 157-165, SRCA.

35. This tract most likely included the family cemetery.

36. A correspondent traveling with the district judge and attorney general in April, 1864, wrote that "The flour mill of Colonel (Ceran) St. Vrain is on the edge of town and run by the waters of the Mora (river)." Cited in Callon (1962), 31. Almost certainly this was the western edge, since immediately east of the road to Guadalupita the river enters a series of serpentine twists. However, less than a mile downstream from the Guadalupita road the old W.G. Gordon Mill of 1906 still stands next to the highway.

37. Coyote Creek flows into the Mora River about two miles east of the current settlement of Golondrinas.

38. Albright (1984), 95,

39. Baptismal Records, Taos Church, reproduced by F.W. Cragin in Cragin Collection, Miscellaneous File A. There is undoubtedly a kinship between Luisa Branch and her family and Alexander Branch, hunter and trapper with Ceran and the other mountain men of the 1820s, but this cannot be confirmed.

40. Taos County Probate Book B-3, 1850-1864, SRCA, p. 27.

41. *History of New Mexico*, 600.

42. St. Vrain to Francisco, June 29, 1864, Working Papers.

43. Mora J.P. Records, 1856-1868, Microfilm Reel 1, December 31, 1864, 366-368, SRCA.

44. Ibid., 191-2.

45. Ibid., September 11, 1865, 196-198.

46. Ibid., May 15, 1866, 299-301. The partnership agreement was to run for five years, from May 15, 1866 to May 15, 1871.

47. Ibid., February 18, 1867, 302-304. This new partnership had the same ending date as the first one.

48. Mora County, New Mexico Records, Indirect Index, Book 1, March 5, 1868, 384-386, SRCA.

49. Ibid., Book 2, August 20, 1869, 203-205.

50. Benedict Marcellin was the second son of Ceran's brother, Domitille, born in Spanish Lakes, Missouri in 1808. Domatille married Nancy Carrico in 1834, in Missouri, where their first son, John, was born. Benedict was known to all by his first two names, and appears in official records as "BM St. Vrain". He was born in Mora in 1836 and died there in 1887.

Chapter 4: The Mills in Santa Fe and Colorado

1. Cragin Collection, Notebook II, p 23; Frazer (1972), 216-7; Frazer (1983), 80.

2. Swordes to Jessup, November 1, 1846, Extracts, Letters from the Consolidated Correspondence File, Office of the Quartermaster General, 1794-1915. RG92, National Archives (hereafter CCF,QM,NA).

3. McKissack to Jessup, September 16, 1846; McKissack to Jessup, April 12, 1847. CCF,QM, NA.

4. McKissock to Jessup, November 11, 1846, CCF,QM, NA.

5. Easton to Jessup, May 5, 1852, CCF,QM, NA.

6. Easton to Jessup, Ibid.

7. Frazer (1968), 122; (1972), 216.

8. Deed Records, Santa Fe County, New Mexico, Book A, 113-4, SRCA.

9. Frazer (1972), 216-7. It is confusing how St. Vrain could attach property if it were owned by the army.

10. See Elder and Weber (1996), 42.

11. Deed Record, Santa Fe County, New Mexico, Book A, June 20, 1853, 200-202.

12. Frazer (1954), 45.

13. The property was once owned by Candelario Martinez, who served in the New Mexico Volunteers and later became a probate judge in Santa Fe. In 1882 a portion of the land was sold to the Santa Fe Water Company, at the entrance to which two millstones are currently on display—perhaps the original ones. In 1920 the property became the home and studio of artist Randall Davey. I am grateful to Mr. Kim Strout, Director of Development for the Center, for providing documents and background information.

14. Duffus (1930), 77.

15. The first recorded water right, in 1851, was the San Luis People's Ditch. Simmons, Virginia (1999), vii.

16. Elder and Weber (1996), 126. Louis B. "Louie" St. James was a miner living in Denver and in partnership with William O. Boggs as Boggs & St. James. They advertised as "merchants of Auraria and Denver, provisions and hardware, and they handle gold dust." Cited in Fiftyniners' Directory Colorado Argonauts, 1858-1859, Pikes Peak Region, Compiled by Henrietta E. Bromwell, Denver, Colorado 1926, accessible as history.denverlibrary.org/research/fiftyniners/S.html.

17. *Rocky Mountain News*, April 23, 1859, p3, c1.

18. Broadwell was one of the many entrepreneurs to enter the gold-fed economy of Colorado Territory. On December 26, 1859, he inaugurated his new hotel on Larimer Street in Denver with a gala Christmas party, and shortly began advertising The Broadwell House: "The subscriber has recently opened this new and commodious Hotel—the largest and best fitted public house in the country—and solicits a liberal share of the public patronage." *Rocky Mountain News*, December 26, 1859, p3, c2; January 25, 1860, p3, c4.

19. *Rocky Mountain News*, February 29, 1860, p2, c1.

20. Larimer (1918), 133.

21. Quoted in Monnett (1996), 49.

22. Larimer (1918), 134. Denver pioneer E.L. Gallatin suggests that Ceran was a silent partner in the original St. James & Boggs firm, with Edward replacing Boggs for a short time, and Col. A.G. Boone then replacing Edward. He confirms Edward's brief tenure with the firm, suggesting that he was released because he was "more fond of the violin than of business." Cragin Collection, Notebook XX, p. 1.

23. *Rocky Mountain News*, May 28, 1859, p.2, c.4.

24. See Chapter 2, n 68.

25. Simmons, Virginia (1999), 96.

26. Simmons, Ibid., 145.

27. Tushar (1975), 15.

28. Easterday was a merchant and freighter who was a partner in the operation of St. Vrain's mercantile business in Taos. In 1858 he had managed Hersch's new steam-powered flour mill in Santa Fe (Elder and Weber 1996, 106).

29. In 1858 Fort Garland replaced the ill-situated Fort Massachusetts.

30. The original contract may be found in *New Mexico Economic Records*, SRCA, Santa Fe. The agreement was witnessed by "T. Mignault" and Charles Beaubien.

31. Easterday continued operation after his partnership with Ceran was dissolved, and finally sold the mill to the short-lived Mormon colony of Eastdale in 1890 or 91. Simmons, Virginia, Ibid., 224.

32. *Rocky Mountain News* Weekly, April 18, 1860, p 3, c 4.

33. *Rocky Mountain News Weekly*, October 8, 1860, p4, c1.

34. Volumes have been written on this and the other Spanish and Mexican land grants. A succinct, if opinioned, version of the Las Animas sequence of conveyances can be found in Joab Houghton's recapitulation in the *Las Animas Leader*, January 9, 1874, p.1, c.3-6. This may be accessed online at www.Colorado Historic Newspapers.org. In February, 1859, St. Vrain had appointed Houghton as his agent and attorney in all land transactions on the grant; Taos County Records, Deed Book A-1, 1852-1882, p 205.

35. Murphy (1972), 39.

36. Miller (1997), 47.

37. *Post Returns, Cantonment Burgwin*, 1855, RG 393, NA. While his unit was at Burgwin from January until transferred to Santa Fe in July, Craig appears on the roster only for January.

38. Taylor (1968).

39. Albright (1984), 97. The date she gives for the appointment is March 22, 1853. At the end of February, however, Colonel E.V. Sumner, commanding the Department of New Mexico, refers to Francisco as sutler to Cantonment Burgwin. Sumner to Wagner, February 28, 1853, LS, M1072, RG 393, NA.

40. Thomas (2002).

41. Albright (1984), 97-8.

42. Frazer (1983), 140.

43. Albright, Ibid., 99.

44. Charles Autobees was an early merchant for Simeon Turley, owner of Turley's Mill in present-day Arroyo Hondo, just north of Taos. Turley's famous "Taos Lightnin'," raw and harsh on the throat and warm in the stomach, was traded along with flour at Bent's Fort and later at the early fort at Pueblo. Autobees escaped death in the Taos Rebellion of 1847, in which Turley and others at his mill were murdered, and later served on the jury which convicted the insurgents.

45. Wooton had a store and a mercantile warehouse on Ferry Street in 1859, but Doyle was the better businessman. Wooton's business, including a hotel built later, failed, and he retired to a farm near Pueblo.

46. Lecompte (1978), 256-258; *Rocky Mountain News*, "Passing On," January 1, 1873, p4, c2.

47. Albright (1984), 100.

48. Albright, Ibid., 115.

49. *Rocky Mountain News*, May 30, 1860, p3, c1. This is the same issue that carried the St. Vrain & Easterday advertisement. Stewart may be Lucian Stewart, one of Ceran's household members in Santa Fe in 1850.

50. The full text of the contract may be found as Appendix B in Albright, 311-313.

51. Joseph Felix was actually the third son, and second by Maria Trujillo, but their first, Matias, born in 1842 in Taos, had not survived a year. Felix had joined his older brother in Mora from school in St. Louis in 1861.

52. Christofferson (1987), 8-9.

53. Christofferson, Ibid., 10.

54. Daigre to Francisco, July 31, 1864, Daniel Working Papers.

55. Felix St Vrain to Daigre , December 15, 1864, Daniel Working Papers.

56. Daigre to Francisco, November 24, 1865, Daniel Working Papers.

57. Daigre to Francisco, Ibid. Theodore Mignault, with whom St. Vrain established a partnership in 1866 to operate a lumber business in Turquillo, north of Mora, became St. Vrain's agent in the Cucharas, much the same as Henry Daigre handled affairs for Francisco. Mignault also apparently managed the Taos interests while Vicente was running the Mora enterprises. Mignault otherwise remains an enigmatic figure. As noted in Chapter 3, there were apparently two Mignaults: Theodore and Tancrede. Unfortunately, the frequent reference to "T. Mignault" fails to clarify the relative roles of the two.

58. St. Vrain to Francisco, June 29, 1864, Daniel Working Papers

59. Working Papers; as noted previously, Colonel Albert Gallatin Boone operated a general store and outfitted Indian traders in Denver, in Westport, Missouri, and later in Council Grove, Kansas. Boone's nephews, friends of Hiram and Felix, were likewise in Westport that spring.

60. Albright (1984), 96.

61. Albright, Ibid.

62. Vasquez (1931), 108.

63. Albright, Ibid., 105.

64. Albright, Ibid., 106.

65. Albright, Ibid., 130-131.

66. Daigre to Francisco, November 24, 1865. Working Papers.

67. Albright, Ibid., 131, 151. The French settler, Beaubois, had been granted the land by Ceran St. Vrain in 1858, among many others, in an effort to settle his grant. When Beaubois was killed in a dispute, Ceran reacquired the land and ranch.

68. 10th, 11th, and 12th Federal Census, respectively, Schedule I: Population. Ceran had apparently given Huerfano land to his daughter and Felix's younger sister, Isabelita, before his death. She was living with her husband, Pedro José Gomez, and their four children in the household adjacent to Felix in 1880. She died on Christmas day, 1900, and is buried, along with her husband, in the same cemetery as are Felix and "Pelegrina" (Huerfano County online records.) Their son, Vincente, is undoubtedly the Jose Vincente St. Vrain who wed Maria Constancia Pino in St. Mary's, Colorado, on November 7, 1898. He would have been 22 years old. St. Mary's is a small settlement thirty miles west of Denver (Marriages, 1897-1900, Huerfano County, Colorado, Book 4, Huerfano County Clerk's Records.)

Chapter 5: Milling and Merchants at Century's Close

1. The will has appeared in several publications, including Broadbent (1987).

2. Felicia Hall, personal communication, February 7, 2009.

3. *History of New Mexico*, vol. II:595.

4. Mora Deed Records, Book 2, p. 317, SRCA.

5. Mora Deed records, Book H, p. 378.

6. Miller (1989), 359.

7. In official documents, the name has alternative spellings, most commonly "Muller." Murphey refers to him as "Miller", Murphey (1972), 29-41.

8. Taos County Probate Book B-3, SRCA, p. 270.

9. In March of 1864, Müller was appointed guardian of Charles' son, Pablo. Taos County Probate Book B-3, SRCA, p. 362.

10. It is noteworthy that earlier in the 1860s, a partnership consisting of Müller, Clothier and Ceran St. Vrain operated a freighting firm that hauled merchandise through the Huerfano

Valley from New Mexico to Pueblo and Denver. See Cragin Collection, interview with John Brown, Walsenburg, December 8, 1907, Notebook VI, p3. It is not unreasonable, therefore, that their Ranchos mill was indeed the old burned mill, refurbished.

11. United States Census, 1870, Town of El Rancho, County of Taos, Territory of New Mexico, Schedule 4, Products of Industry, p 1.
12. Cited in Miller (1989), 151.
13. U.S. Census, 1870, Ibid.
14. Taos Probate Book B-3, pages 284, 286, 296.
15. Miller, (1989), 151.
16. U.S. Census, 1870, Schedule 4, La Cueva Pricinct No. 5.
17. F.W. Cragin interview with Joseph B. Watrous, Las Vegas, NM, Feb. 14, 1908. Cragin Collection, Notebook VI, pp 23-24.
18. U.S. Census, 1870, LaJunta Precinct No. 11, Mora County, Schedule 4.
19. Miller (1989), 8, 10. Kroenig had been one of the original settlers on St. Vrain's Las Animas grant under Charles Autobees in 1853. See Lecomte (1978), p 229.
20. Register of Contracts, QMG, RG 92, M1, 1871-1876, NA.
21. Miller, Ibid, 369.
22. Hooker (1996), 21f.

Chapter 6: Mill Architecture and Technology

1. Reynolds (1983), 17.
2. Weber (1996).
3. See, for example, Fox, *et. al.*, (1987).
4. Bishop (1868), Vol. 3: 271.
5. James Leffel, Springfield, Ohio, patented his initial turbine wheel in 1845. The improved "Double Turbine Water Wheel" in 1862 brought the James Leffel and Company fame and profit well past the mid-20th Century. The James Leffel and Company Collection, Special Collections and Archives, Paul Laurence Dunbar Library, Wright State University, Dayton, Ohio.
6. Albright (1984), 114.
7. Albright, Ibid.

Chapter 7: The Excavations

1. This section is taken from the original field report by Randy Stice and Michael Wendorf.
2. Wetherington, 2008.
3. This section is taken from the original field report by Jeanne Fillmore, Laura Kersten, and Connie Gordon.
4. Tierra Blanca is a gypsum-rich white clay which is mined in several parts of Taos Valley and elsewhere. It is frequently peppered with tiny slivers micaceous muscovite. A nearby source is in the valley just south of Ranchos de Taos.
5. This section is taken from the original field report by Glenda Barber, Marsha Dekan, and Sara Dorsey.

Chapter 8: The Artifacts

1. Fike (1987), 204.
2. Fike, Ibid., 205-6.
3. Fike, Ibid., 225.
4. Fike, Ibid., 110.
5. All examples discussed were diagnosed by reference to "Glass Factory Marks on Bottles", at myinsulators.com/glass-factories/bottlemarks2.html. Accessed 1/14/09.
6. Fontana and Greenleaf (1962), 95.
7. Fontana and Greenleaf, Ibid., 92. Ironstone was introduced to the U.S. in the mid-19th Century and widely used at military posts on the western frontier, due to its durability.
8. Fontana and Greenleaf, Ibid., 105.
9. Fontana and Greenleaf, Ibid., 106.

Bibliography

Abel, Annie H., ed., *The Official Correspondence of James S. Calhoun* (Washington: Government Printing Office, 1915).

Albright, Zella Rae, *One Man's Family: the Life of Hiram Vasquez* (privately printed, Colorado, 1984).

Anonymous, "The Charles Bent Papers," *NMHR* 30:340-352 (1955); 31: 75-77, 157-164 (1956).

Arrott Collection, Donnelly Library, New Mexico Highlands University, Las Vegas, N.M.

Baker, T. Lindsay and Billy R. Harrison, *Adobe Walls: The History and Archeology of the 1874 Trading Post* (College Station: Texas A&M University Press, 1986).

Ball, Durwood, *Army Regulars on the Western Frontier, 1848-1861* (Norman: University of Oklahoma Press, 2001).

Barreiro, Lic. Antonio, in Carroll, H. Bailey, and J. Villasana Haggard, trans. and eds., *Three New Mexico Chronicles* (New York: Arno Press, 1967).

Baxter, John O., *Las Carneradas* (Albuquerque: University of New Mexico Press, 1987).

_____, *Spanish Irrigation in Taos Valley* (Santa Fe: A study prepared for the New Mexico State Engineer Office,1990).

Beck, Warren, and Ynez Haase, *Historical Atlas of New Mexico* (Norman: University of Oklahoma Press, 1969).

Bennett, James A., *Forts and Forays: A Dragoon in New Mexico, 1850-1856*, Clinton E. Brooks and Frank D. Reeve, Eds, (Albuquerque: University of New Mexico, 1996).

Bishop, John L., *A History of American Manufacture from 1608 to 1860* , 3 Vols. (Philadelphia, E. Young, 3rd ed., 1868)

Bloom, Lansing, "Barreiro's *Ojeada Sobre Nuevo Mexico*", *NMHR*, **3:86, 1927**.

_____, "The Rev. Hiram Walker Read, Baptist Missionary to New Mexico," *NMHR* 17:113-147, 1942.

Broadbent, Edward H., *Ceran St. Vrain: 1802-1870* (Pueblo, Colorado: Pueblo County Historical Society, 1987).

Bromwell, Henrietta E., comp., *Fiftyniners' Directory Colorado Argonauts, 1858-1859, Pikes Peak Region*, (Denver, Colorado, 1926). Available online at history. denverlibrary.org/research/fiftyniners/S.html. Accessed March 4, 2009.

Callon, Milton W., *Las Vegas, New Mexico, the Town That Wouldn't Gamble* (Las Vegas: Las Vegas Daily Optic, 1962).

Carson, William G.B., ed., "William Carr Lane Diary (Conclusion)," *NMHR*, 39:274-332 (1964).

Carter, Harvey L., "Marcellin St. Vrain," in Hafen, LeRoy R., ed, *French Fur Traders and Voyageurs in the American West* (Spokane: Arthur H. Clark Company, 1995), 283-287.

Census of Canada, 1901.

Census of the United States, 1850, 1860, 1870.

Christofferson, Nancy, *Francisco Fort and the early days of La Veta, 1862-1876,* (Privately printed, 1987).

Condition of the Indian Tribes: Report of the Joint Special Committee, U.S. Congress, U.S. Govt. Printing Office, (1865).

Daily Rocky Mountain News.

Daniel W. Working Papers, Archives and Special Collections, Colorado State University Libraries, Fort Collins, Colorado.

Deed Records, Santa Fe County, New Mexico, Book A, SRCA.

Dictionary of American Biography, published under the auspices of the American Council of Learned Societies (New York: Scribner, 1935).

Duffus, R.L., *The Santa Fe Trail* (N.Y.: Tudor, 1930).

Dunham, Harold H. "Ceran St. Vrain", Hafen, LeRoy R, ed., *Mountain Men and Fur Traders of the Far West* (Lincoln: U. of Neb. Press, 1982), 146-165.

Earl Fischer Database of St. Louisians, St. Louis Genaeological Society, available at www.stlgs.org/publicationsSurnamesEarlFisher.htm. Accessed April, 2009.

Elder, Jane Lenz, and David J. Weber, eds, *Trading in Santa Fe: John M. Kingsbury's Correspondence with James Josiah Webb, 1853-1861* (Dallas: Southern Methodist University Press, 1996).

Extracts, Letters from the Consolidated Correspondence File, Office of the Quartermaster General, 1794-1915. RG92, National Archives.

Federal Census, Santa Fe, New Mexico, Schedule I, 1850.

Fierman, Floyd S., *Guts and Ruts: The Jewish Pioneer on the Trail in the American Southwest* (New Jersey: Ktav Publishing House, Inc, 1984).

Fike, Richard E., *The Bottle Book* (New Jersey:The Blackburn Press: 1987).

Fontana, Bernard L., and J. Cameron Greenleaf, "Johnny Ward's Ranch: A study in historical archaeology," *The Kiva* 28:1-115 (1962).

Fox, Anne A., Lois M. Flynn, and I. Waynne Cox, *Archaeological Studies for the San Antonio Channel Improvement Project, Including Investigations at Guenther's Upper Mill (41 BX 342)*, Center for Archaeological Research, The University of Texas at San Antonio Archaeological Survey Report, No. 136 (1987).

Francis W. Cragin Papers, *Early Far West Notebook* series, The Pioneer's Museum, Colorado Springs.

Frazer, Robert W., *Mansfield on the Condition of the Western Forts, 1853-54* (Norman: University of Oklahoma Press, 1954).

_____, Ed. *New Mexico in 1850: A Military View* (Norman: University of Oklahoma Press, 1968).

_____, "Purveyors of Flour to the Army, Department of New Mexico, 1849-1861", *NMHR*, 47: 213-238 (1972).

_____, *Forts and Supplies: The Role of the Army in the Economy of the Southwest* (Albuquerque: University of New Mexico Press, 1983).

Garrard, Lewis H., *Wah-to-yah and the Taos Trail* (Norman: University of New Mexico Press, 1955).

Gorenfeld, Will, "The Battle of Cieneguilla: the Historical Record," in Wetherington, Ronald K., and Frances Levine, eds, Battles and Massacres on the Southwest Frontier (Norman: University of Oklahoma Press, *in press*).

Hafen, LeRoy R., "Fort St. Vrain," *The Colorado Magazine*, XXIX: 4 (October, 1952): 241-243.

_____, Ed., *Mountain Men and Fur Traders of the Far West* (Lincoln: U. of Neb. Press, 1982).

_____, Ed, *French Fur Traders and Voyageurs in the American West* (Spokane: Arthur H. Clark Company, 1995).

Hanosh, Eugene J., *A History of Mora, 1835-1877*, M.A. Thesis, New Mexico Highlands University, June 1967.

History of New Mexico: Its resources and people, 2 vols (Los Angeles: Pacific States Publishing Company, 1907).

Hooker, Van Dorn (with Corina Santistevan), *Centuries of Hands: An Architectural History of St. Francis of Assisi Church* (Santa Fe: Sunstone Press, 1996).

House Journal, Aug 7, 1848, 30 Cong. 1 sess.

Huerfano County online records at files.usgwarchives.org/co/Huerfano/cemeteries/ butte.txt. Accessed March, 2009.

Huerfano County Clerk's Records; online at files.usgwarchives.org/co/vitals/marriages/ bridemz.txt. Accessed March 2009.

Kenner, Charles L., *A History of New Mexican-Plains Indian Relations* (Norman: University of Oklahoma Press, 1969).

Larimer, William H. H., *Reminiscences of General William Larimer and of his Son William H. H. Larimer* (Printed for private circulation, Lancaster, Pa.: Press of the New Era Printing Co., 1918).

Las Animas Leader.

Lavender, David, *Bent's Fort* (Lincoln: University of Nebraska Press,1972).

Lecompte, Janet, "Ceran St. Vrain's Stone Mill at Mora," Ms., Cultural Properties Review Committee, State Planning Office, Santa Fe (n.d.).

_____, *Pueblo, Hardscrabble, Greenhorn* (Norman: University of Oklahoma Press, 1978).

Letters by the Ninth Military Department, Department of New Mexico, and the District of New Mexico, 1849-1890, Microcopy received 1102, RG 393, NA.

Letters Sent by the Ninth Military Department, Department of New Mexico, and the District of New Mexico, 1849-1890,Microcopy 1077, RG 373, NA.

Marshall, Thomas M., "St. Vrain's Expedition to the Gila in 1826," *Southwestern Historical Quarterly Online*, (1916),19(3):2. Available at www.tshaonline.org/publications/journals/shq/online/v019/n3/article_3.html. Accessed July 2008.

McNierney, Michael, *Taos 1847* (Boulder: Johnson Publishing Co., 1980).

Miller, Darlis, "Los Pinos, New Mexico: Civil War Post on the Rio Grande", *NMHR* 62:1-31 (1987).

_____, *Soldiers and Settlers: Military Supply in the Southwest, 1861-1865* (1989).

_____, Ed., *Above a Common Soldier, Frank and Mary Clarke in the American West and Civil War, 1847-1872* (University of New Mexico Press, 1997).

Monnett, John H., *Colorado Profiles: Men and Women who Shaped the Centennial State* (Niwot: University Press of Colorado, 1996).

Mora County J.P. Records, 1856-1868, Microfilm Reel 1, SRCA.

Mora County, New Mexico Records, Indirect Index, Book 1, SRCA.

Mumey, Nolie, *Old Forts and Trading Posts of the West*, (Denver: Artcraft Press, 1956).

Murphy, Lawrence R., *Lucien Bonaparte Maxwell: Napoleon of the Southwest*, (Norman: University of Oklahoma Press, 1983).

_____, "Charles H. Beaubien," in Hafen, ed., *French Fur Traders in the American West* (Spokane: Arthur H. Clark Company, 1995).

New Galenian, May 30, 1832, "The Killing of Felix St. Vrain," reproduced online at www.wisconsinhistory.org. Accessed July 2008.

New Mexico Economic Records, Santa Fe: State Records Center and Archives.

New Mexico Passport Records, Santa Fe 1827-1828, Manuscript Collection 184, Folder 1, Center for Southwestern Research, Zimmerman Library, University of New Mexico.

New York Times, June 29, 1859.

Papers of the St. Louis Fur Trade, Microfilm, Part 1, Reel 12, frame 537, *Chouteau Collection, 1752-1925*, Missouri Historical Society.

Parish, William J., *The Charles Ilfeld Company* (Cambridge: Harvard University Press, 1961).

Post Returns, Cantonment Burgwin, RG 393, NA

Reynolds, Terry S., *Stronger Than a Hundred Men: A History of the Vertical Water Wheel*, (Johns Hopkins University Press,1983).

Risch, Erna, *Quartermaster Support of the Army: a History of the Corps, 1775-1939* (Washington, D.C.: Center for Military History, Government Printing Office, 1989).

Roberts, David, *A Newer World: Kit Carson, John Fremont, and the Claiming of the American West* (NY: Simon & Schuster, 2000).

Rocky Mountain News, Vol XI, November 1, 1870.

Santa Fe Gazette.

Simmons, Marc, "Santa Fe's Street Names," available at www.sfaol.com/history/street. html. Accessed January 2008.

Simmons, Virginia M., *The San Luis Valley: Land of the Six-Armed Cross* (Niwot, University Press of Colorado, 1999).

Sopris, W.R., "My Grandmother, Mrs. Marcellin St. Vrain," *Colorado Magazine*, XXII:2 (March 1945), 62-68.

Stevens, Frank E., *The Black Hawk War* (Bowie, MD: Heritage Books, 1993).

Taos County Records, Deeds, 1853-1869, Book A-1, SRCA.

Taylor, Morris F, "Capt. William Craig and the Vigil and St. Vrain Grant, 1855-1870," *Colorado Magazine*, XLV/4:301-321, (1968).

_____, *First Mail West* (Albuquerque: University of New Mexico Press, 1971).

Thomas, D.B, *From Fort Massachusetts to the Rio Grande* (Thomas International, Washington, D.C., 2002).

Tushar, Olibama López, *The People of "El Valle": A History of the Spanish Colonists in the San Luis Valley* (Privately printed, 1975).

Van Ness, John R. & Christine M., *Spanish & Mexican Land Grants in New Mexico & Colorado* (Manhattan, Kansas: Sunflower University Press, 1980).

Vasquez, Hiram, "Experiences at Fort Bridger, With the Shoshones and in Early Colorado," *The Colorado Magazine*, VIII:3 (1931), 106-108.

Voelker, Frederic E., "William Shirley (Old Bill) Williams," Hafen, ed., *French Fur Traders and Voyageurs in the American West* (Spokane: Arthur H. Clark Company, 1995), 193-222.

Watts, Martin, *The Archaeology of Mills & Milling* (Charleston:Tempus, 2002).

Weber, David J. *The Taos Trappers* (Norman: University of Oklahoma Press, 1971).

_____, *The Mexican Frontier, 1821-1846* (University of New Mexico Press, 1982).

_____. "Sylvestre S. Pratte", Hafen, LeRoy R, ed., *French Fur Traders and Voyageurs in the American West* (Spokane: Arthur H. Clark Company, 1995), 258-269.

_____, *On the Edge of Empire: the Taos Hacienda of los Martinez* (Santa Fe: Museum of New Mexico Press, 1996.

Weekly Rocky Mountain News. Available at www.coloradohistoricnewspapers.org.

Wetherington, Ronald K., *Cantonment Burgwin: the Archaeological and Documentary Record*, NMHR 81:391-411 (2006).

William C. Carr Papers, Missouri Historical Society, St. Louis.

Index

(References to illustrations are in **bold**)

CPSIA information can be obtained
at www.ICGtesting.com
Printed in the USA
FSOW02n0639270317
32371FS